STILL BREATHIN'

THE WISDOM & TEACHINGS OF A
PERFECTLY FLAWED MAN

BRENDEN M. DILLEY

Copyright © 2013 Brenden M. Dilley

Published by Rock Bottom Publishing, LLC

Printed in the United States of America

Still Breathin': The Wisdom and Teachings of a Perfectly Flawed Man
Written by Brenden M. Dilley
Edited by Amy L. Weicker

Note: This book is intended only as an informative guide for those wishing to learn more about life, love, relationships, sex, mental health, fitness, spirituality and parenting. Readers are advised to consult professional coaches, counselors or doctors before making drastic life changes. The reader assumes all responsibility for the consequences of any action taken based on the information presented in this book. The information in this book is based on the author's research, experience, education and observations. Every attempt has been made to ensure that the information is accurate; however, the author cannot accept liability for any errors that may exist. The facts and theories presented herein are subject to interpretation, and the conclusions and representations made may disagree with other interpretations.

Please direct media inquires and event booking requests to
StillBreathinBook@gmail.com

ISBN-10: 061589545X
ISBN-13: 978-0615895451

DEDICATION

---

*For my children, Sophia Rose,
Jasmine Nai'a, and Phoenix
Alexander... we finally made it.*

CONTENTS

ACKNOWLEDGMENTS

Rarely is anything worth accomplishing done without the assistance of hundreds, if not thousands, of silent contributors. The culmination of this book is certainly no different.

First and foremost, I must thank my hero and number one fan, my mother, Lisa Kitter. You have sustained me through so much as a man that I sometimes forget you were also the one raising me as a child. I could not have asked for a more perfect human being to have brought me into this world and to have shaped my mind and heart. You are and always will be the best mother a son could ask for.

I must also take time to thank my children: Sophia Rose, Jasmine Nai'a and Phoenix Alexander. You have provided me the inspiration and the "why" necessary to overcome every single obstacle I have faced. I have never been more in love than I am with the three of you. Each of you has uniqueness and "light" that I most certainly look forward to watching develop as the years pass. No matter what happens in this life, Daddy loves you all and is so proud of who you are. You're simply too amazing for words.

I had a bit of an interesting time growing up and didn't have the best relationship with my father, Mark Dilley. However, as I grew into a man and we both found peace within ourselves, our relationship has flourished, and I feel so blessed to have you in my life. You're the one who taught me the value of a job well done, to take pride in my work and that being sloppy has consequences. I can honestly say that my ability to multi-task and learn is a direct result of your innate ability to do seven things at once… and excel at them all. Thank you, for this is one of my greatest assets as a man.

Grandma... I love you. You're an amazing woman who has taught me so much through the trials and tribulations you have overcome. You're far stronger than anyone probably realizes, and I want you to know I recognize your brilliance as a soul. I feel so fortunate that you're providing the same grandmotherly love to Sophia, Jasmine and Phoenix as you did for me.

I would also like to acknowledge my mentor, John Lupypciw. No person walking this Earth has taught me more about business and the ability to persevere through adversity than you have. Your most valuable gift may just be the sheer will with which you function. You're completely fearless in your decision making and in who you are as a man. The attention to detail and uncanny ability to "create" whatever you set your mind to is something I have never observed at the level at which you do it. I also would be remiss if I did not mention your advice in the area of women. You taught me to "lead" in a relationship and not to be afraid to be a "man." I have never observed a man walk the line of strong and driven while thoughtful and giving more so than I have with you and your treatment of my mother. God bless you for delivering to her the person she waited over forty years to find.

This book was also made possible by my friends, numerous clients and "enemies" who played a unique role in my life. Thank you to all of my friends who offered an intent ear while I struggled, helped me out financially (GP,) and gave so much to me while the only thing I had to offer in return was becoming the man I told you I would be. Thank you to all of my clients for allowing me to be part of your journey. Through your struggles and accomplishments, I was able to better know myself. Everything that I taught you was returned tenfold by what I learned by being in your lives. I am so proud of all of you who continue to grow, change and persevere.

I would also like to thank my "enemies." There may not be a more responsible person for the publishing of this book than you. I know that I am not perfect and that I have hurt many of you. For this, I am sorry. However, I want you to know that I was able to grow and develop thanks in large part to you. Our experiences together provided me the opportunity to fail. It provided the pain, anguish and suffering necessary for me to develop the character, humility and love needed to succeed. God bless all of you for these gifts, for I could not have become the person I was meant to be without you.

I would also like to extend a very heartfelt thank you to my fantastic team of editors and designers for this project...

Amy Weicker, your direction and watchful eye has allowed a raw manuscript to become a beautifully put together book. Thank you so much for your honesty and insane work ethic. I could not have completed this on time without you.

Vicki Pankhurst, I cannot thank you enough for taking the grammatical and punctuation atrocity that was my initial manuscript and turning it into something that could actually be read and worked on. I am in your debt.

Brandon Robinson, you have captured the idea I had in my head for a book cover to a "T." Thank you so very much. I am so proud of the work you have done.

INTRODUCTION

I would like to start by saying a sincere "thank you" to you, the reader, for having chosen to give me your most valuable of commodities when you chose to read this book... your time.

I would like to make clear what this book "is" and what "it isn't." When I began compiling my different writings and thoughts, I had but one goal: to be as authentic, sincere and honest as possible. The majority of self-help "gurus" like to present themselves as something far more superior than they actually are... flawed. This book contains every part of me: my love, my anger, my sense of humor, my insecurities, my confidence, my sexuality, my empathy and my brutal honesty. Any editing was done primarily to correct my terrible grammar and to clean up run-on thoughts.

However, this book is not "clean." I did not allow it to become a bastardized, commercial version of my vision. There are passages that will comfort and inspire. There are also many writings that will be about as subtle as a punch in the face and will force you, the reader, to question your own personal beliefs... and that is my intent. My goal is not to be perceived as "enlightened" or "advanced" in any way, shape or form. I wish only to present myself as "whole."

I am a man who is completely at peace, yet wages constant battles about the human experience. I realize that much of what I just wrote is paradoxical and may be criticized by writers and critics whom are far more educated than me, and I'm OK with that. They're not the intended audience. I have no need for "smart" men and women's opinions. This book was written for the rest of you. It was written for the single mother or father struggling to make ends meet. It was written for the introverted academic whose intelligence has made intimacy a seemingly impossible experience. It was written for the bully whose own demons and torments compel him to spread his anger.

This book wasn't written for the wealthy, out of touch business person. It was specifically written for those who are still in the struggle and are looking for hope... a spiritual life preserver.

This book contains pieces of my soul that I will not apologize for here in the introduction, nor at the conclusion. Those that are meant to get it, will. Those that aren't will have stopped reading by now.

Truth be told, the idea for this book started over a decade ago. Its actual culmination has been delayed for the better part of a decade due to a few personal flaws that include, but are not limited to: procrastination in my younger days, the decision to have three children before the age of thirty, poverty and some success – but most of all, it was the belief that I had not "suffered" enough. It had been my belief that you cannot reach or teach anyone anything from an authentic place without having cultivated a significant amount of empathy through your own personal failures.

I set off to fail in as many different ways as possible – not intentionally, but rather subconsciously. During that time, I learned much about human behavior, faith, intelligence, love, hate, forgiveness and loyalty. I am not an expert "psychologist," and although I fancy myself an intellect, I am fully aware that at times, I sound like I'm completely full of shit. If I were to label myself as anything, it would be an "expert" on the human condition. I've got three children from two "baby mommas." (I hate that saying; it's crude and incredibly crass, but it is an unfortunately accurate phrase.)

I was married once and learned valuable lessons, like not to marry someone after knowing them for 10 days simply because they've got a heart shaped booty and a sexy Texas drawl! I still can't believe that one didn't work out! I also learned to not let your self-worth be determined by others... especially people who, in fact, hate themselves. They will only project their own visceral hate of self onto you.

Other things to remember are that a relationship can be prolonged by a steady dose of mind blowing orgasms and laughter. (Pro-tip for men: to keep a woman around long-term, make her laugh during the day and scream at night.)

At this point, you might be asking, "But Brenden, if that works, then why have your previous relationships failed?" The answer is simple: women in their twenties are completely insane. I do, however, think that as they age, they chill out and "allow" themselves to be happy. God bless them in their twenties though, because they're the most irrational, immature, insecure creatures on the planet. Throw in the over-inflated sense of entitlement and unwillingness to ever be alone, and you've got a recipe for an overly attractive pseudo-intellectual who believes that she can attention whore her way to the top!

That being said, men in their twenties aren't much better and certainly don't do anything to dispel the insecurity their women experience. Being a disingenuous man-whore isn't doing much to represent the male gender.

The new breed of "player" isn't just after sex or your pocket book. He wants more. He needs you to love him. His insecurities are derived from a lack of self-love and a life without purpose. He cannot give himself the acceptance he so desperately needs, so he dates women – often multiple women – in seek of approval.

Both sexes are responsible for the suffering of one another… and that's OK. As a matter of fact, it's perfect. It's why people in their thirties are so much more humble and authentic. (Well, if they've outgrown their previous behaviors, that is. Truth is, some people are just inherently fucked up, so there are exceptions.)

But I digress. My goal isn't to highlight the failures of humanity. I'd more or less just like to show that it's a natural occurrence of the human experience. Failure is a progression that allows for all of us to become more empathetic and authentic people. It is necessary and while we should acknowledge it, we should not fear being the victim, nor the culprit of these experiences. Eventually, you will have had the opportunity to wear both "hats" at different stages of your life, and from that, you'll hopefully develop a significant amount of character and ultimately, find peace.

I fully anticipate my past failures being a point of criticism given the content of this book. I'm attempting to lay out ALL of me in the hopes that by the end of having read this book, you'll feel like you can identify with my struggle. My number one goal is to assist anyone who reads this in becoming more than you were before you picked up this book.

THE LUCKY HORSESHOE IN MY ASS

HOW I "MADE" A MILLION DOLLARS IN 2009

Nobody is dropping a million dollars in your lap. Your "King/Queen" isn't showing up on a magical steed. Rather, financial success is gained by doing small things every day over an extended period of time. Love is developed often not in one single moment but rather, a series of events that lead to the discovery and development of love. The Universe will challenge you to see if what you desire is consistent with whom you are. The question you must ask yourself is, "Are my hopes and desires consistent with my daily action?" If the answer is "no," take the necessary steps to forgive yourself for your imperfection and commit to living a life that is consistent with your dreams.

This story begins back in the summer of 2006. My then "partner" (the mother of my two daughters) and I had begun the process of refinancing our home in Arizona. We had lived in the house since the winter of 2005, and we were eager to do some upgrades. My oldest daughter, Sophia, was turning one, and we wanted to finally finish refurbishing the house.

At the time, we were both involved in real estate and financing, so we began the upgrades while our loan documents were still being approved. As many of you remember, getting a loan in 2006 consisted of verifying a pulse and getting yourself down to the title company to sign. There wasn't much risk since everything seemed to be on the up and up.

Knowing that I was slammed with work, my ex took it upon herself to secure the financing and ensure that everything was all handled correctly. We had close to fifty thousand dollars in equity to pull from, and our intention was to put about fifteen thousand dollars toward upgrades and keep a little cash for ourselves.

I'd also like to point out that during the summer of 2006, while this was occurring, our relationship was fucked up at best. We were fighting daily. That's not an exaggeration. Every. Fucking. Day.

I remember coming home and just sitting in my driveway, and as excited as I was to see my daughter, I dreaded having to deal with her mother. (Sounds like a healthy relationship, huh?) Looking

2

back, I still can't believe the number of hours, tears and stress I wasted on this completely ridiculous relationship.

On one hand, I'm thankful for having had the experience, because I learned so much, and it made me a more patient and empathetic man. On the other, I want to go back and kick the twenty-four-year-old version of me square in the balls. Can you imagine? You're twenty-four years old, you hate your life, and for what? For some stupid, co-dependent relationship that you're convinced you're stuck with because "we have a baby." Fuck that shit, never again.

The reason I mention the status of the relationship is because it is one hundred percent going to tie in the next three years of my life and ultimately, my million dollar realization. Our relationship was bad, we had about fifty thousand dollars in equity, and I had trusted her to ensure that the financing went smoothly.

Can you see how this might turn into a problem? We began the repairs, and our landscaping was in the process of being done, our carpets were all being replaced, and we were painting and texturing throughout. The home was really coming together, and we were both excited to finally have something to be proud of.

In the days leading up to our "signing," the contractors we used were beginning to ask for their money, and we were assuring them that the bank was going to be funding any day now.

Finally, on a Thursday, my girlfriend called and told me that the documents had made it to the title company, and they were ready for us to sign. She let me know that she would be signing during her lunch break, and that I could go down after work to sign my portion.

I should have sensed something was off based on the way she was laying out these plans, but I was incredibly naive and didn't pay attention to the clues. After work, she came home and let me know it went smoothly, and we talked briefly about the entire transaction. She told me that the title officer was waiting for me and, "It should go really quickly because it's only one or two documents to sign."

Immediately, my bullshit detector went off!

"What the fuck do you mean I only have one or two documents to sign? The last time we secured financing, it was thirty plus pages of signatures and initialing."

"Well… umm… I mean, your credit score wasn't quite as strong as mine, and leaving you off of the loan will save us about a hundred dollars a month. You only need to sign the documents removing you from the title."

This woman had refinanced me off of the house. She ensured that we began the work so that I would be pressured into signing my name off of the only investment I'd ever had, in order to pay out the vendors.

I was left with a decision. (Strangling her to death was not an option, although it had crossed my mind at that point.) I could say, "Fuck you!" and not sign the documents. Then I would have to deal with the vendors and try to come up with the thousands needed to pay them.

My other option was to sit for a moment quietly in my car and ask God for a little guidance. Within a few minutes, I had my answer… and three years later, I would realize "why."

I drove down to the title company and signed my name off of that house. The day I did that was the absolute beginning of the end of our relationship, and it would set up the next seven years of my life.

Eventually, we worked through that particular deceit and continued on in our dysfunctional relationship. Seven months later, we were given the opportunity to purchase an investment condominium at well below the market price. Since I didn't have the necessary payment history, I couldn't qualify for the loan. She, however, could. She secured that investment on her own, using the equity from "our" house.

In the spring of 2007, we found out that we would be welcoming our second daughter later that year. We immediately began shopping for a larger home to live in. Eventually, we found a stunning home for three hundred and fifty thousand dollars that had everything we wanted. It was a dream home and we loved it. Not only that, but we were fortunate enough to have a strong offer on our home as well.

There was one problem. I had no legal ability to decide whether we sold or not. She had all the power, as I no longer was on the title of the home. The offer was for five thousand less than we were asking, and it was a cash buyer. We could officially wipe our hands clean of the house and have a significant down payment on our dream home.

"No! I either want a full price offer, or I'll just keep it and rent it out!" she shouted.

"Baby, the market is shifting. I don't think it's a good idea. You're being greedy. We need to sell this house and move on," I countered.

"Listen to me. I'm the OWNER of this house, and I'm not selling it. Period," she argued.

I relented. I knew she was fucking up. I had a bad feeling about this, and something inside of me warned that a wave was coming. For a year, we lived like gods. We had three homes, two of which were investment properties. Well, technically, **SHE** had three homes, but whatever...

Our life was all about abundance and family. The relationship was still on life support, but the birth of our beautiful second daughter, Jasmine, seemed to breathe new life into the romance.

I don't have to tell you what happened in 2008. Bank after bank failed. She got laid off but was a very hard worker and managed to piece together enough business as a realtor to stay afloat. I had launched my personal training business prior to the crash and was having some early success. Things, while difficult, seemed to be survivable.

However, she got it into her head that we would be better off relocating to Northern California and renting a home from her family. She failed to mention that...

  a) The city we were moving to was an absolute shit hole.
  b) The economy there was infinitely worse than in Arizona.
  c) She was going to transform into an even more difficult spouse once we were near her family, and she felt empowered to act like an idiot.

Now, to her credit, I was a fucking moron. I went along with all of this shit and didn't really question it. I had been acting like a know-it-all prick and had alienated my family to the point that we were hardly speaking. I allowed myself to buy into the idea that "the grass is greener" in a town full of white trash meth-heads near Modesto, California.

At this point, you're probably thinking, "How the hell does this end up making him a million dollars in 2009?"

Let me explain… her "investment" condo was already in the process of being foreclosed on. (That's one hundred and eighty thousand dollars.) Our previous home – that I had also encouraged her to sell – was also being threatened with foreclosure, following a few missed payments. (There's another two hundred and fifty thousand dollars.)

The only property that was still afloat was our primary residence, thanks to a renter who paid a year's worth of rent up front. (There's a three hundred and fifty thousand dollar mortgage.)

If you're keeping track, that's roughly eight hundred thousand dollars worth of mortgages, and we aren't even going to discuss the lines of credit against them.

I officially ended things and moved out on May 8, 2009. She blew through the remainder of the rent money before the end of the year. I had left with nothing and gave her the contents of our bank account. All I had was my tax money and some cash I'd borrowed from my family. She was eventually able to short sell our dream home, but she was far from out of the woods. Judgment after judgment was levied against her, and the creditors were piling up to the tune of nearly one million dollars!

My phone didn't ring. Nobody called or harassed me for any mortgages, lines of credit or otherwise.

On that June day in 2006, when she had allowed fear to dictate that she fuck me out of our asset and the equity held, there were other powers at work. As I continued through the rest of that year and was unable to buy real estate, those same powers maintained their poise. Not having the ability to be on any of those loans has set me up for the next decade.

For three years, I thought that **I** was the one who got screwed out of a million dollars in real estate. I couldn't have been more wrong! Yes, I eventually did hit rock bottom financially and had a car repossessed and a credit card sent to collections… but that was it. I had both of those issues straightened up within twenty-four months.

However, when you fuck the bank out of a million dollars, ignore court orders to appear and never make an effort to settle, those issues don't just disappear.

It's been four years since I left, and she still doesn't have the ability to borrow ANY money. She can't get a car loan. She can't even get a Sears card, let alone a home loan.

This story isn't meant to be a "ha-ha" toward her. I sincerely empathize with what she's going through. I paid my cosmic debt from 2009-2011.

She chose to delay that pain and is only now beginning to feel the effects of those decisions, as her car was repossessed six months ago, and she's had to move several times over the last year.

I was able to avoid one million dollars in debt – debt that would have all but ensured I would never be able to buy a home again – thanks to a thirty second decision in 2006. I'll be honest. If you were to talk to her, her family or her husband, that story gets a significant twist to it. It's completely about how I screwed her into one million dollars worth of debt and left her financially destitute. Nobody ever bothers to ask HOW or WHY she ended up in that position.

I'll be even more honest with you now… I still don't give a single fuck. I have ZERO guilt associated with what eventually transpired. She and I both know the truth, and while she may not accept it, it does not make it any less true.

The bottom line is that when you put deceit, hate and vengeance into the world, you will eventually have to reap what you've sown. I've never sought any type of revenge for the things that occurred in my life, nor for her having screwed me out of our house.

Ultimately, it was the greatest financial blessing of my life, and to this day, I count it as my first million.

If you're dealing with stress or experiencing financial strain, and you're worried... STOP! It's going to be fine. You can't see the entire playing field. Have some faith in the process of life. Keep putting good out into the world and allow the Universe to balance things out for you.

I'm Wrong

AND I COULDN'T BE HAPPIER

The phone never rings,

The door never knocks,

Losing track of time,

While staring at the clock.

An eye toward the future,

With a firm hand on the past,

Stuck in between moments,

That rarely ever last.

But what if they did,

Would you, could you accept the truth,

That all you've got are fuzzy memories,

And a scarred heart that bears the proof?

I am significantly more relieved when I'm "wrong" versus when I'm "right." That might sound silly, but it's true. The validation that comes from being "right" is short-lived and temporary. However, the lessons learned and humility gained from being "wrong" can last a lifetime.

Many men and women invest so heavily in being right that even when they've been proven wrong, they still continue to argue. Conceding defeat or accepting the truth isn't an option.

Ah, "truth." Now we're talking. The truth is all any of us are ultimately seeking. The truth has a ring to it and a way of settling down situations and putting us all back on our path. The truth doesn't need to be flaunted or rubbed in.

Saying "I'm sorry" or "I was wrong" does not make you a weak person. It also doesn't necessarily validate or make the other person right. The realization of our own wrongdoing could easily be described as the admission of a lesson learned. Let's not misunderstand though… it takes a significant amount of courage and character to admit when you've done something wrong. I'm finding that the older I get, the higher the stakes when it relates to mistakes.

The moral decisions I'm faced with almost daily now dwarf the decisions I was making in my younger years. It's during these times that your character is truly tested.

I'd like to share the biggest "wrong" I've ever perpetrated. My goal as a human being is to live the most authentic life possible. In pursuing that goal I've found that it's critical to maintain a skeleton-free closet at all times. The honesty with which I'm about to tell this story will promise to keep my closet clean, long after I'm gone.

I'm going to preface the story with this statement: Shame, for a truly loving human being, is far and away the most intense of the emotions in the human experience.

I was married in December of 2010. I did not think this decision through; my girlfriend and I had begun talking via webcam and the phone only nine months prior. She resided in Texas and I lived in Northern California. We had met through a prominent bodybuilding website and sort of just stumbled into one another's lives. We talked nearly every single day, exclusively as friends for the first seven months.

I enjoyed her immensely, and she knew I wanted more. However, she wasn't open to anything initially, so I accepted that I had just made a really great friend. It should also be noted that at this particular juncture in my life, I was NOT in a good place. I was making bad or wrong decisions constantly. I hadn't quite gotten my feet planted after my prior separation a year and a half earlier, and because of my unwillingness to "heal" properly, I was half a man.

Here's a pro-tip: If you're in a bad place and struggling on multiple fronts in life, do NOT make any life-altering decisions. Do everything in your power to delay those decisions until you've sorted out your other issues.

Eventually, our friendship would turn romantic, and in December of 2010, I flew her to stay with me. We spent the majority of that month together, including Christmas at each other's family homes and then New Year's together. Just prior to New Year's, we got this retarded idea in our heads to go down to the court to get married. This was beyond stupid, but the combination of us both being in bad places and the ridiculous level of sexual attraction resulted in us going through with it.

Almost immediately, the marriage was doomed. She moved to California with me only six weeks later, and we kicked off the most dysfunctional five-month relationship that **ANYONE** could imagine.

My wife got pregnant in May of 2011. Our marriage was in full-blown crisis mode at this point. We were both elated and terrified by this revelation. At the time, I was still spending an unbelievable amount of money on attorney fees from my child custody battle for my daughters.

As the months wore on, we made the decision to relocate back to Arizona. The benefits were a more stable working environment, being near my family and having a greater support system for both of us. My wife's family also lived in Arizona, which made the move extremely attractive to her.

The one and only **GLARING** downfall was that I would be moving away from my daughters. However, thanks to the most corrupt justice system in the state of California, I had already been robbed of the majority of my parenting time anyway.

I went from being a very hands-on, fifty percent physical custody dad to an "every other weekend and holidays" dad. However, this move did provide some benefit to the girls. They would more frequently be afforded the chance to see their grandmother, with whom they are both extremely close. They would also get to continue developing their relationship with their great-grandmother, who we're so blessed to still have in our lives.

Eventually, I figured out a reasonable custody arrangement. It's basically the same schedule that I had while residing in California, but now I would fly back on those weekends to see them every month.

Our move was stressful for both of us. She was three months pregnant, and it was the dead of summer. Her pregnancy wasn't going very well, as she was constantly bed-ridden with morning sickness. In addition, our relationship had disintegrated during the previous four months. Upon arriving in Arizona, I immediately began my new job. The relief of finally being near family was short-lived, and a week later, the relationship ended.

I had been out of town and came home to find her family at my house. We had only been living there a week, so none of her belongings were unpacked. I think we both knew intuitively that we were nearing the end of our "run" as a couple.

As I entered our bedroom, she was laying on the bed crying. I wasn't sure what was going on, and nobody was really saying anything to me. She informed me that she was going to her father's house. I was exhausted, having spent the previous eighteen hours driving, and said that I understood and proceeded to take a shower.

When I came out of the shower, she was gone. It appeared that several of her boxes and suitcases were gone as well. I was elated. I can't even begin to describe the sheer relief that washed over me. Our relationship had been so toxic up to that point… to have it "end" so quietly was a blessing.

My assuming it "ended" is where I went wrong. I had misinterpreted her saying, "I'm leaving and staying with my dad," to mean, "I'm leaving permanently and staying with my dad."

A few days went by before we spoke. I was still stressed out, learning a new job, and I figured she needed time to gather her thoughts.

She called me later that week, and it quickly turned ugly. It was exactly the type of behavior that had led to our separating in the first place. Having exchanged verbal barbs for a few minutes, she eventually hung up on me. I didn't think much of it and assumed that this is how "divorces" sort of go.

That afternoon, I took the liberty of changing the locks on my house. I did not trust her, as I had already been privy to what she was capable of doing. She had removed the majority of her belongings when she left anyway, so I didn't think it was a big deal.

It was a big deal...

She came back days later, for what I thought was to get the remainder of her items. We sat and talked at my kitchen table for the better part of an hour. She wanted to continue the marriage; I had one hundred percent checked out. I was not interested in continuing the insanity that had been our relationship.

Devastated... she left. On that day, I learned that there are certain things you just can't come back from.

I did not feel "guilt" or "shame" in that moment. I did not believe I was wrong for having stood my ground. In my mind, I was doing the right thing. She was staying in a safe, stable environment with people who loved her. Neither of us were being exposed to any more dysfunctional fighting.

My thought was that we'd give one another some space for a few weeks, then plan for the remainder of the pregnancy. I was of sound mind and my intentions were pure.

What I wasn't yet aware of, however, is the fact that her family is a bunch of fucking lunatics. Her brother is a violent, steroid abusing teenager, and her father isn't exactly the most imposing figure. I did not know that she was living in chaos while at her father's home.

We had exchanged emails and instant messages but not phone calls. I had changed my number and wasn't going to provide her that number until she calmed down. She did not make me aware the nonsense going on with her family. I was wrong for not having given her my number.

By September, she had broken all communication with me. I emailed regularly, inquiring about the status of the pregnancy as well as her wellbeing. Weeks turned into months before I would get a response.

Seven weeks after my wife moved out… I met someone. The spark was instantaneous and hot. We were drawn together in a way I had only experienced once before. with the mother of my daughters. Our "relationship" started as a friendship. Every single day, we would spend time together after work and the gym. I was hooked. So was she.

I shared everything with her. I told her I was still married and that my wife was four months pregnant. I told her I had two daughters from a previous relationship. I shared of the poverty I had endured and the decisions I had made.

She never judged me. She accepted all of it and only wanted to learn more. She was an angel. She was my angel. This woman had come into my life and offered something I had never experienced in my entire life... stability and respect.

Love blossomed. She was my best friend and lover. I was an emotional basket case, and she put me back together. Her entire focus was on illuminating all of the positive aspects of me as a person. She did not judge me, and through that non-judgment, I was able to start making rational, sound decisions.

The one glaring problem was that I hadn't properly dealt with my prior relationship. It remained an open wound for both me and my wife.

My wife's "silence" was quickly erased upon learning of my new relationship. She emailed me and informed me that she had left the state, that our son would never know me, and that I would never be a part of his life in any way, shape or form. She told me that I was disgusting for having started a new relationship while she still carried my child, despite her having disappeared for two months.

I was beyond conflicted. Slowly, that cold, lonely feeling of shame washed over me. "Was I wrong? Did I not fight hard enough for the marriage? Had I not taken all of the steps necessary to reach her?"

The truth was that I had done the best I could with the information I had at the time. This happens in multiple phases of life for all of us. We make decisions that we believe to be the best and are only allowed to learn from those wrong decisions by making them.

The guilt and shame began to consume me. I started to second guess the love I had found. I began to feel "unworthy" of such a pure connection.

"How could anyone love me?" I thought. My entire life, I've done my best to strive for "win-win" situations. It's a part of my genetic make-up. I had done this with my wife and failed in epic fashion. Her insanity was terrifying, and a large part of me wasn't able to think beyond the "crazy."

My inability to deal with the guilt and shame corroded the first "honest" and "healthy" relationship I had ever had. I informed my love of this happening, as she knew I had been acting distant. I told her I loved her, but I needed to get my mind right. I couldn't continue with the relationship with this hanging over my head.

Before I continue this story, I'd like to make one thing clear. I do not, never have and never will "regret" leaving my wife. I knew I didn't love her. I knew it was an unhealthy, emotionally draining, train wreck of a relationship.

My guilt and shame came from having handled it the wrong way. My ex-wife had challenges that go way beyond the "norm" as far as psychology goes. I was not equipped to deal with them and did not fully understand the extent of those challenges.

None the less, I felt undeserving of my new love and amazing friendship. My ex-wife finally contacted me in January – mere weeks before my son was born. She hinted that she might be open to returning to Arizona with our child. The one and only caveat was that I could not have the woman I'd been seeing involved in my life. She told me that if she was still in my life, that she would never consider returning with my son.

Our conversations were still premature, and while I had scaled back the relationship with my love, I was not going to cut her out of my life without my ex-wife showing more than a "willingness" to return.

My son was born on February 6, 2012. I was not present. He's the only one of my children that I wasn't there to see born. He was a week old when I first learned of his birth.

Eventually, my ex-wife agreed to visit and allow me to see my son for the first time. They flew to visit on March 21st. He was six weeks old and absolutely adorable. I let the woman I was seeing know that I wouldn't be able to see her for a week, and that I would talk to her when the visit was over.

I was being selfish. I was wrong for treating her this way. This woman deserved better.

My number one focus was getting my son back! Everything else was just collateral damage. I did not have the luxury of being true to my feelings about her or our relationship.

The visit went well and at the end, my ex-wife said that she would return. Her only requests were that we go to marriage counseling and that I not have any contact with the woman I had been seeing.

My ex-wife didn't, doesn't and never will understand just how much I loved that woman. She was everything I ever wanted in another human being. Our friendship was incredible. My attraction to her was second to none. Her mind and maternal instincts pushed me to become a better/stronger man.

I was faced with a decision that I would not wish upon my worst enemy. The choice was between my son and the love of my life. There was no other option; I would not be given a second chance.

The decision, while being one of the most painful of my life, was also one of the easiest. I am a Dad. This is far and away the most important job I've ever taken on. I am not a dead beat, and I am not irresponsible. I spent one week with my son, and there wasn't a chance in hell that I was going to have a third child living in another state.

I chose my son.

I called my love on the day my ex-wife and son flew home. She had no idea the emotional bomb I was about to drop on her. I informed her that not only could we not keep seeing one another, but that we couldn't even be friends. It killed her. It killed me. Even as I type this right now, I can feel the emotions of that day.

There are times in your life when you will be faced with decisions that are going to test you. The only losers in this situation were the adults. I was devastated because I was losing the love of my life. She was devastated for the same reason.

My ex-wife would eventually be devastated because she had used our child as leverage to sneak back into my life, and it would come back to haunt her.

The only winner was the one that mattered most... my son, Phoenix.

The guilt and heartbreak would eventually be washed away with the realization that my son would grow up with both of his parents involved in his life. He would get to experience what it means to be my son and to be a part of our special family.

He would not have to ask questions later in life, such as...

"Who is my real dad?"
"Where does he live?"
"Why don't I ever get to see him?"
"Why doesn't my dad love me?"

The only blessing to come out of the boneheaded mistake of marrying my ex-wife is our amazing son. The silver lining from the entire **wrong** decision is the most brilliant, physically/mentally advanced baby I've ever had the opportunity of knowing. Needless to say, I don't regret this marriage at all.

The numbers of times I've been wrong in my life are too many to count. I am proud to say that my heart has always been in the right place, and those wrong decisions have **ALL** assisted me in becoming a more thoughtful and loving human being.

I lost the love of my life and gained a child. I know that in my lifetime, I'll have the opportunity to love like that again. Even though at times the pain of that decision still stings, it quickly evaporates when I'm with my son.

You Thought Your Job Sucked

A Lesson in Humility

Your life is out there. You want money? Hustle. You want love? Give love. You want accolades? Be memorable. Nobody owes you anything. It's up to you to put yourself out there fearlessly. Put in the work. Earn the success, love and recognition. The time is ticking off of the clock. Our tomorrows are promised to no one. Stay present. Grind.

Everything that happened yesterday, last month, last year doesn't mean anything. It's gone, lost to the sands of time. All you've got is this. Right here, right now. Make the changes necessary for success in this moment. Think about whom it is you want to become and be that person NOW. Do not allow life to dictate who you are. That's a choice you make while lying in bed awake in the moonlight.

We've all had shitty jobs. I'm talking soul sucking, jam a pencil in my ear, "Fuck this! I wonder if I can do internet porn," dead end jobs.

Typically, we work these shit-ass jobs out of necessity: because we're "in between" careers, starving college students, or we're just desperate for employment. There is no shame in doing what must be done to put food on the table. There is, however, an immense amount of embarrassment attached to some of these fucked-up job positions. I'm going to share with you my experience and why it should make your job seem a little less terrible.

It was the summer of 2009. I had just left my first wife. (OK, we weren't married and most would call her my "baby-momma," but whatever.) I was living near Sacramento, California, and it was easily one of the hardest-hit regions during the economic downturn. We had nine hundred plus people lining up around the block at the new "In N Out Burger," waiting to submit their resumes and hopefully get an interview. Times were desperate, and everyone was taking any job available, as we were all fighting to stay above water.

I was no different. When I left, all I had was a handful of in-home personal training clients, my tax return money, and a few items that had been donated by friends and family. It was terrifying yet exciting, as I knew I was embarking on a new portion of my life.

I called Craigslist ad after Craigslist ad, trying to line up something, anything for gainful employment. My tax money was going fast, and I still had shared fifty/fifty physical custody of my daughters. They would spend exactly half the week with me and the other half with their mom.

My goal was to not only find a job, but to locate one that would have hours that worked with my schedule as a single father. Given the economic conditions, it was next to impossible to find a job filling those needs. That was until I saw an ad on Craigslist that read:

"Local resort restaurant hiring servers/dishwashers at lake front establishment."

Immediately, I called. They informed me that positions were in fact available, and I should come down to the resort and fill out an application. I was THRILLED! I knew if I could get a serving job, it would mean immediate cash, and I could hopefully get a schedule that worked with the girls.

My first interview happened to land on a day when my mom was in town visiting. She and a friend of mine were out running errands prior to my interview, so they decided to drive me to the resort and wait in the car. As I left them in the parking lot and entered the main entrance, I began to sense things were "off." It had an eighties porn type of decor and it smelled funny.

I introduced myself to the front desk woman and she smiled, handed me an application to complete and told me I could sit in the waiting room "facing the volleyball court." I happily took the application and walked over to the table that was facing this massive wall of windows overlooking a beautiful manmade lake and volleyball court... and at that moment, I saw something I was **NOT** prepared to see.

There were about ten people on the volleyball court, playing and having a wonderful time. They were decked out in knee braces, headbands, visors, sunglasses... and that's where the normality stopped. They were playing... naked.

All of those accessories and not a single shirt, shorts, or jockstrap were seen that day. It's funny because the very first thought I had wasn't, "Oh fuck, they're naked!"

It was... "Wait, why the fuck are you worried about a knee brace when you're playing volleyball with your cock and balls dangerously flopping about!?" The irony had me nearly in tears from giggling.

"What the fuck! Where the hell am I?"

Slowly, other "customers" began entering the building to register for the weekend. They too carried purses, wore hats, sunglasses and flip-flops... with their tits and wieners dangling about.

My mind was so blown that I literally couldn't even comprehend the moment. Yet, I was desperate for work, and if I was going to have to see a bunch of fat, old, naked people to make a buck... by God, I was going to do it.

The Interview:

Eventually the restaurant manager comes down and sits with me at the table (he was clothed, thank God). We talk for a few minutes and fortunately for me, he was a big, overweight gay man. I immediately turn on the old "Dilley Charm" and talk my way into a waiter position despite having no experience.

The manager informs me that our dress code is "polo shirt with khaki shorts." I will be working the "breakfast shift" every weekend, and we'll go from there.

Excitedly, I exit the building to find my mom and friend sitting in the car laughing hysterically. Not ten minutes before I came out of the building, a golf cart with four naked old guys went driving past their vehicle while my mom and friend were mid-conversation.

You know… life is funny like that. You're scraping the bottom for work. You've got no dignity left in place. You **THOUGHT** you were going to keep your embarrassing, shitty new job a secret from your friends and family. Yet, that's when the Universe sends eight hundred pounds worth of fat, geriatric, sweaty man balls skirting past your mom and best friend in a golf cart.

Fuck my life.

Well, that's a first:

I arrived for my first shift at my new job at six in the morning, sharp! I was thrilled to be working and even more excited that I would be going home with cash in hand at the end of the day. My new manager showed me around the restaurant and began explaining the nuances of the job and protocol. The restaurant wasn't open yet and since I had arrived so early, there really weren't a lot of guests out and about.

I had been psyching myself up all morning, and I felt prepared for the onslaught of naked bodies that can only be described as aging silly putty that has begun to melt, dry and crack in the California sun.

The manager also informed me that I would be "shadowing" one of the other waiters for the first half of the day and that the second half of the day, I would be on my own. I was fine with this arrangement, as I figured it would afford me the opportunity to adjust to the horrors that awaited me.

I was wrong.

Our morning shift went off without a hitch. Naked body after naked body entered the restaurant and left without much happening. After the fourth or fifth table, I started to become more comfortable helping out, taking drink orders and bringing food.

My eyes still struggled to remain horizontal, but since below the neck was occupied by the sobering reality that I too would one day look like this... and even worse, I'd be nailing women that look like this, it did make it slightly easier to focus on faces.

My new method of avoiding naked bodies was quickly destroyed.

"Brenden, go ahead and take these cocktails out to the pool. There is a woman out there who ordered them with a blue sun hat. She already paid and is waiting for them."

"OK, no big deal," I thought. I'll just take these drinks out there, keep my head down toward the ground, and everything will be fine.

At this point, I should mention that I had not anticipated the "logistics" of said pool. The pool had this decking that was massive, to accommodate all of the many leather-bound bodies that enjoyed getting their daily dose of melanoma. The layout had this sort of "stair" effect.

When I walked outside, I immediately saw a blue hat in the distance tanning on her stomach. I started off in her direction and was confronted with these "step-ups" that surrounded the pool. I hadn't really thought my strategy of staring at the ground all the way through before heading out the doors. I did not adjust for the "step-ups."

As I got closer to where I had seen the blue hat, I focused intently back on the ground, trying to gauge the distance from myself to her using only quick glances up.

I knew I had arrived when I caught a glimpse of blue out of the top of my vision. The problem was that the step-ups had sort of elevated her naked body in such a way that while the blue was at the top of my gaze, my actual focus was directly on her lower body.

She was laying face down, completely spread eagle with her legs far apart. This was the first time I had ever encountered another human being and had come face to face with their asshole prior to actually having seen their face. Her chocolate starfish seemed to be basking in the morning sun.

To make matters worse, I sort of stammered out, "Ma'am did you order some drinks?" while my gaze was still on her bunghole. I must have caught her by surprise, because it sort of winked at me just before she rolled over to confirm that the drinks were indeed hers.

The four dollar tip did help ease the pain of that first encounter. It is, however, a drop in the hat for the years of therapy I'm certain to require in my future.

Live. Laugh. Love. Puke.

Keep the Change:

With day one on the books, I returned home with fifty-five dollars in tips and a sense of accomplishment. I didn't make much, but it was enough for groceries and a little gas for the car. My second day went significantly smoother than the first one. I hadn't met anyone else "butthole first" and was getting the hang of taking orders and remembering the specials.

All was well through the morning breakfast crowd, and I was looking forward to finishing up my day with the afternoon lunch rush. Table after table filled up, and the pungent scent of sun block, grilled cheese and sweaty ass crack permeated throughout the restaurant. This was the first really hot day of the summer and the customers were doing anything to escape the sun, even for just a few minutes. We stayed busy all through lunch.

Finally, toward the end of my shift, I had a "table of one" sit in my section. She can only be described as a massive, mid-forties woman with a "white-trashy" kind of charm. Her massive gut was dwarfed by the triple E tits that rested peacefully on top of it. Her pancake nipples could have fed a small village of starving African children... all at the same time.

Quickly, I took her order and since she was one of my last tables, I was really doing my best to give her great service. I had been busy all day and was trying to make every last nickel going into the week ahead. Her food and service were impeccable. Satisfied with her meal, she headed to the register, where I would meet her to close out her tab.

"Sixteen dollars and fifty-seven cents," I chimed.

"Oh, is that all?" she responded.

This next part is as accurate as I can describe the event that followed. With her left hand, she cupped the bottom of her Sasquatch-sized breast and lifted. Her right hand reached underneath her massive mammary and pulled out the wettest, stickiest twenty dollar bill, which I can only guess had resided there all morning as she baked in the sun like a Thanksgiving turkey.

She slapped it down on the counter next to the register and with a grin, chirped, "Keep the change!"

"What in the actual fuck?" I thought.

I needed that money, but there was no way in hell I was going to grab it off of that counter. Being the quick thinker that I am, I summoned over my manager, Brian.

"Hey Brian, do you think you could break this twenty?" I asked, as I looked down at the soaking wet bill.

"Yeah sure," he exclaimed while reaching for it. "Wow, was this in someone's balls all morning, it's soaked?" he asked.

"Ha! I don't know, man. You never know with these people," I shot back.

Brian took that disgusting twenty dollar bill and left me four crisp five dollar bills on the counter.

Victory was mine.

Rock Bottom:

The entire summer went on like this. Not once did I go into that job and not walk out with an assortment of stories. The customers, for the most part, were sweethearts. They also happened to be extremely generous. (Or perhaps they just didn't like carrying change, since they didn't have any place for it.)

I was and am so thankful for having had that job. However, it was beginning to wear on me. The kitchen staff was sub-par at best, and the food was getting progressively more disgusting. As the food began to suck, the tips suffered.

In addition to coping with this shit-ass job, I was also dealing with a child custody battle. I was slowly but surely losing everything I owned and had my car repossessed.

As much as I hated the job, it was all I had left. My in-home training clients had reached their goals for the wedding they were attending, and these naked, fat fucks were my only source of income.

For that reason, I kept a smile on my face and soldiered on with a humble heart. You do not know what you're made of until you've achieved success in a respectable career, only to follow it with accepting money from under a fat woman's tit and bringing drinks to a butthole err... I mean a woman lying by the pool.

My humbleness was going to be tested at least once more on this day. I had a couple sit in my section that already looked to be in a bad mood upon arriving. They were my typical, mid-forties, fat, balding, pierced up, tatted up nudist customers.

He ordered an omelette; she had the cottage cheese and fruit. Minutes ticked off the clock as I waited for that Goddamn omelette to come up the dumbwaiter. Each time I peeked my head out of the wait station, I could see this guy growing angrier.

"DING!"

Finally, my food had come up. I snatched it out of the dumbwaiter and raced it to their table. I dropped it off and refilled their drinks while I was there. I hadn't gotten more than a few steps from the table before this fat fuck had bit into his disgustingly cold omelette.

"What the fuck is this shit!?" he bellowed. "I waited forty-five fucking minutes for this nasty fucking omelette, you stupid motherfucker. Why would you serve me this slop? I should have you fired for trying to bring me out this disgusting shit!"

Now... the old "me" would have stopped this guy halfway through his tirade by punching him in his fat fucking mouth and then dumping the omelette on his head. I am not someone that people get away with yelling at.

It doesn't matter if you're my boss, customer or whomever; I'll give you respect, but I demand the same. If you want to get in the ring with me, that's my favorite place to play.

But this wasn't the old me. This was a struggling single father with two little girls and nothing left… who just had his car taken away, borrowed all the money he could and was hanging on by a string.

He was saved. He was saved by the previous seven years of my piss-poor spending. He was saved by my daughters, my hungry dogs and my landlord. He was saved by a man who hit absolute rock bottom.

That was my hundred percent rock bottom moment. I had been a respected professional, a published fitness author and had done millions of dollars in financing while working in construction lending. Yet there I stood, taking the tongue lashing of a lifetime from a fat, lazy, rude, shrimp dick, ugly wife having jerk-off.

Humility washed over me. This was a turning point. I knew I wouldn't be the same after that day. It changed me. I don't know that I've ever been more proud of myself in my entire life than I was at that moment.

I quietly apologized, took the food from in front of him and called my manager over to smooth things over. I had put my children, priorities and goals firmly ahead of my ego and pride. I haven't had much pride since that day. I do not look down upon men and women who do what they have to do to survive. I get it. I understand. I've been there and done it.

Hopefully, hearing about the horror that was my shit-ass rock bottom job can help bring a smile to your face about your situation. Even better would be if it causes you to treat others with more empathy, as none of us know the people we're encountering on a day-to-day basis.

I'd like to thank that gentleman for his behavior that day. He gave me something that had eluded me up until that point... humility.

WHAT'S WITH THE F***ING CURSING?

Are you down to your last dime, your last friend, your last hope? Keep fighting. There is only one way to survive this jungle, and that's to embrace the scars, heartache and strife. I'll happily jump in the foxhole with you if you've got the stomach to accept my advice.

The solution to most of life's problems is love. However, every once in a while, a lion is necessary to thin the herd... to keep things on an even keel, and that's where I come in. Honor the lions in your life. Their methods might not always be the most politically correct, but they get shit done.

Yesterday, I was having a wonderful conversation with my lovely grandmother, and the topic of my writing came up. My grandma enjoys my writing and has for as long as I can remember. However, yesterday she was quite upset about the frequent use of curse words.

After having a somewhat lengthy conversation with her, I realized that perhaps I should offer an explanation as to why I choose to use curse words in my material.

Because... I fucking feel like it.

Ha! Just kidding... that's not it at all. The real answer is a little more complicated, and hopefully I can clear up any misconceptions about my potty mouth and use of curse words.

My mother is/was a motivational speaker and author. My mom and I have very similar personalities, and while she isn't nearly as crude as I am and doesn't curse as much, she does have a sick sense of humor. Back in 2002, my mom released one of her most successful audio series (that would later become a book) ever. It was titled, "The Game of Life for the New Millennium."

This audio/book series was a tribute to one of her favorite authors, Florence Scovel Shinn, who had penned a book titled, "The Game of Life and How to Play It," back in 1941. At this point you're probably asking yourself...

"What the hell does this have to do with using curse words?"

Well, I'll tell you. That book was/is a very "spiritual" book. The wisdom and teachings were phenomenal, and up to that point in her career, she had been extremely professional and not so controversial. The release of that audio series was met with a lot of skepticism as well as criticism because the content was contradictory to traditional religious teachings.

After the audio series was released, people would always approach my mom at speaking events and other business functions with a sense of awe – wanting to be near her because they believed she had some "divine" power.

Now I don't know about you, but I think that's a lot of fucking pressure. People now had an expectation of "who" she was and the persona that was being projected was that of some kind of spiritual guru. No crude jokes on stage. No occasional curse words while speaking. No more aggressive business tactics. No more making "human" mistakes or being a jerk because she didn't sleep.

Nope. They believed she walked on water, and it made her resent some of the success she experienced. She wanted to put the genie back in the bottle because it wasn't a realistic ideal to live up to. Hell, I don't know how spiritual "masters" (whatever that means) can do it. You're telling me that they never get cut off in traffic and snap!?

The point I'm trying to make in regards to my potty mouth and use of curse words is that I do not ever want to "elevate" myself above anyone. I do not ever want to paint myself into a corner through my own creativity.

I allow the world to see my cruder side so that I'm able to write spirituality, self-help and other empowering material without killing my ability to drop an "F" bomb from time to time in my personal life or in my material.

I don't buy it when someone says they're above this type of expression. I'm not saying all of those "gurus" are full of shit but... well... they're full of shit. It might just be my own interpretation of life, but I do not believe we were sent here to be perfect or to pretend to be.

How the hell are you supposed to develop any humility if you don't allow yourself to act like a dick once in a while? Let's be honest, we're all capable of misrepresenting ourselves and saying some stupid shit that's going to hurt those around us.

The only difference is that I'm one hundred percent honest and sincere about it... and upon realizing that I'm wrong, I apologize immediately. Lesson learned.

"But Brenden, you're alienating your audience when you curse! It makes you look unintelligent and classless."

I get this one a lot too…

Well, I've got news for you. For every single person who thinks that my use of curse words is alienating someone, there are ten other people who would NEVER read a "self-help" book or blog and then keep coming back to read more.

Because I do not pretend to be anything more than an experienced man with a gift for writing and a direct line to "source," they happily read my work.

I'm not trying to appease any particular audience. I don't necessarily WANT to target people who've already got their shit together. What the fuck good is that going to do for any of us? It doesn't mean I don't appreciate all of you who read my stuff… but you're already implementing the lessons and teachings.

My goal is to reach that late teen, early twenties kid who is on his/her way to douchebag status and doesn't have any "teachers" to relate to. His/her only mentors are musicians and asshole celebrities.

I want the single mothers, ex-convicts, strippers, druggies, alcoholics, lost and hopeless souls to be able to read my material and not feel alienated. They're a significantly larger portion of society and they, above everyone else, require the most love and attention.

That, my friends, is why I curse. That is why not all of my writing is geared toward love, spirituality and enlightenment. This process of "life" is a very deliberate path. I write how I write because I am attempting to connect with struggling individuals, in the form of my sincerity, authenticity, flaws and humor.

THE FACTS OF LIFE
THE ELEPHANT IN THE ROOM

There was a day, two years ago, when I woke up in my freezing ass cold house, and the only thing keeping me and my girls from being popsicles was an electric blanket. That nasty house had no heater and no air conditioning. In my mind, not only did I know that I would climb out of that horrible environment, but I knew that I would re-emerge with something very few have achieved... the ability to overcome anything. It's only a memory today, but so help me God, if it all went away tomorrow, I can say with one hundred percent certainty that I would not only come back, I would be stronger than ever before.

I've been contemplating how I'm going to write this. If I don't accurately illustrate my point, it's going to appear incredibly negative and "demotivating," which is the polar opposite of the message I'm trying to convey.

I'll just come out and say it: not all of us are going to make it. As a matter of fact, there is a significant chance that the majority of us won't make it.

What do I mean by "make it?" Simple… depending on the size of your ambitions, there will be a direct correlation to your odds of achieving success in life. However, in life, the word "success" can only be determined by the person seeking it.

The good news is that there will inevitably be a few who do make it. This is where we're going with this chapter. I am not attempting to dissuade, dump on or otherwise remove you from the path you're following toward your hopes and dreams. My goal is in explaining and hopefully pointing out, that sometimes as we seek a particular outcome, goal or dream, we've got to pay close attention to the path we're on and the signals we're receiving.

I've seen quite a few men and women get stuck pursuing a particular career, mate or goal and end up getting lost. Years tick off the calendar. Stress, self-doubt and all sorts of shit that will make you sick later in life, begins to set in.

Goals are healthy. Dreams are a must. Yet you, the seeker of said goals and dreams, are responsible for altering and/or updating them as you continue your pursuits. I would say that the majority of the endeavors I've set out on have magically led me toward paths I would never have fathomed. It's amazing! I have only a handful of "goals" in life, and I'll share them with you briefly.

Goal #1 - Publish a book

I did not put a timetable on this goal, as the quality and end result far outweighed the desire to publish trash. Truth be told, I've been writing this book for the better part of a decade. The goal was to put out a book at some point in my life. This means I've had no reason to rush. Much of what I'm sharing here and online every day is the wisdom and words I've been writing since I was eighteen years old. The difference is that my "teachings" are now supported by actual experiences and stories that I've lived.

Goal #2 - Stay fit my entire life

This is the one that most people had a hard time understanding when I was younger. As time has gone by and I've gotten older, more and more people understand what I meant. I never had the desire to get on a stage and compete. I don't really stress over how "big" or "small" I am. My goal from the beginning was to stay healthy, muscular, athletic and young, and so far so good.

Goal #3 - Children

I've written quite a bit about my kids, so I'm not going to spend much time on this one. Obviously, I've achieved this goal and am probably done making babies... (until I'm seventy-five and I've got a twenty-five-year-old girlfriend who wants a few.)

Goal #4 - Become legendary

This is far and away my most ambitious goal. The odds of achieving it are stacked against me, and that's OK. Life is not meant to be lived on the sidelines. You're meant to attempt and pursue goals and dreams that force you to stretch.

I do not wish to become "legendary" in my life for simple egotistic reasons. Admittedly, it would feel good to reach some semblance of critical acclaim, but it will not leave me with discontent if it doesn't happen.

I've wanted to play a significant role in positively affecting the world since I was a little boy. I have always enjoyed teaching those in my life about the things I've learned and assisting them in their lives.

The greatest wisdom I have learned in my life is that I am at my happiest when I am serving and helping others. I take great pride in seeing others achieve their goals, finding love, losing weight and rediscovering their brilliance.

"But Brenden, why are you telling us we're not going to succeed!?"

Your goals are your own, and you can't let me or anyone else tell you that you aren't going to succeed. For all I know, you might all make it. The point I'm trying to make is that some goals aren't meant to be achieved.

I can't even begin to count the number of times I've imposed my will on the Universe in pursuit of a particular goal, and then proceeded to ignore the ominous signs (some of my romantic endeavors would be great examples,) and had it eventually blow up in my face. Flexibility in life is critical to a happy existence.

I had a number of other goals I used to pursue. Yet, over time, I realized that they were not consistent with my passions or purpose in life. Thus, I let them drift by the wayside, and I refocused on the goals I just listed.

Our goals and dreams must be consistent with our daily action, mindset and purpose. If you're striving for money exclusively, rather than actually embracing a purpose, you will fail. It's not a matter of "if," it'll be a matter of "when."

If you earnestly pursue passions, the end result will grow less important. The path takes precedence, and you're able to be more content and happy every single day. Being on a journey rather than obsessing about the destination will inevitably lead to a greater sense of achievement and "wholeness."

My goal of becoming legendary or famous might never come to fruition. Yet, it is the pursuit of this goal and my sheer enjoyment derived from it that makes it worth dedicating my life to.

YOUR LIFE SUCKS

BECAUSE YOU'RE STILL IN IT

One day, you will wake up and realize everything you worked for, prayed for, fought for, bled for, cried for... is happening. It didn't occur by accident. It wasn't luck or chance. The result was earned through hard work, unwavering faith and a willingness to recognize your fear... and then pursue your dreams anyway.

Most men and women won't make the hard decision. They will not discuss uncomfortable feelings. They'll keep things buried. They'll feign interest and ambition, but they cannot fake depth. You cannot fake sincere interest and warmth. There is no substitute for courage and bravado.

Decide what you want and never ever stop until the world has succumbed to your will.

That terrible attitude, negative outlook and the excuses that you've created for the narrative of your life are following you around like a giant dark cloud. People can see it coming from a mile away. It wouldn't matter if I picked your ass up and dropped you off in the most stunningly beautiful location in the world, surrounded by gorgeous men/women... you would still fuck it up.

Do you want to know why?

The reason is because you will not have altered your perception of the world. You will still believe that your life is a result of being a victim. You will continue disempowering yourself by allowing others to dictate how you feel about you.

Life is itself inherently beautiful. Life is energy. Life is the sun, the moon and trees. Life is flowers. Have you ever actually **STOPPED** and looked at just how incredibly beautiful your life really is???

Perhaps if you resided in some impoverished corner of the world, you "might" have a legitimate gripe. However, if you're an American… I will slap the absolute piss out of you for bemoaning your existence on this Earth. Life is and always will be a gift. The odds that not only would you be the one who made it through to the egg, but more importantly, you would be born in this country, during this moment in history (with modern medicine, technology and overall tolerance… yeah, we use to burn witches,) is absolutely inconceivably fortunate!

You are at this very moment reading the thoughts, wisdom and teachings of a human being who is assumedly hundreds if not thousands of miles from your location. From this exchange, you're able to extrapolate out how fortunate you are to be alive and just what an amazing thing life can be!

Not only that, but by having this exchange via the internet/books, you're able to address those personal psyche problems anonymously. No ridicule from friends and family for being a whiny little bitch. No judgment from co-workers and significant others for reading a "self-help" book.

Nope… it's just you and me. You're free to take the information I'm giving you and begin enjoying your life, or you can leave it — and nobody will know the difference. The point is that this moment in time has afforded you an incredible opportunity to exchange ideas across the world.

You're lucky. You're the most fortunate human being in the history of the planet. If you can:

a) Read this
b) Have the Internet
c) Can get up and walk to the bathroom

You officially qualify in the top percent of humans in existence as far as "luck" is concerned.

The only way you are going to experience the beauty of life is to stop obsessing about what's wrong with it. Nobody is responsible for your happiness or perception of the world... but you. Life is funny like that; just when you think your life is at the center of the Universe, someone comes along and reminds you that your problems are minuscule in comparison and puts your entire existence back into perspective.

LIVE FEARLESSLY...
DIE CONTENT

Fear is your most constant enemy. To be fearful of friendships, fearful of intimacy, fearful of criticism, fearful of being alone, fearful of getting hurt, fearful of making a mistake, fearful of the future, fearful of getting fat, ugly, sick, poor and the list goes on.

Relax. Learn to exhale that fear. The most exciting parts of life are when we're entering the unknown and have an opportunity to witness all of the miracles that this planet has to offer. Don't get caught up in fear. You're going to die anyway, so you might as well have some kick ass memories. Create some new friendships; don't worry about expectations and perceptions.

Stay present in your own life. Surround yourself with people who allow you to feel loved and fully in the moment. Invite friends in who challenge your growth as an individual and force you to stretch your beliefs and mind.

What if I told you that you couldn't fail? What if I told you that the word "failure" doesn't mean anything until you give it meaning? Failure is similar to "beauty" – it's in the eye of the beholder. I've done "insane" things in my life. Now is probably a good time to reiterate that I married my ex-wife after spending only ten days with her. (Can you believe that didn't work out!?)

Want to know a secret? I regret none of it. I could have died multiple times throughout my twenties and would still have lived a full life.

I could be gone tomorrow and my legacy will live on through my children, books, relationships, friendships and life experiences. I live my life fearlessly. Always have, always will. Living fearlessly means living free, and freedom is what makes me happy. For many, freedom (especially mentally) is an esoteric idea that is beyond comprehension.

They judge based on their rules, expectations and experiences. I'll be the first to admit I've been guilty of this. Most people will "judge" because they care and don't want to see someone they care about getting hurt. However, we must always remember that when the people in our lives are living fearlessly, they're going to choose their own experiences. Whether they turn out "good" or "bad" is not for us to decide.

None of it is coming with you – your degree, your raise, your car, your house, your debt, your STDs, your pictures, your money, your regrets, your pain, your anxiety, none of it. It's all gone the moment that last breath has been taken. (Except for your debt... they're going to go after your family for that shit.)

The top five "regrets" of people on their death beds have been reported as follows:

- I wish I'd had the courage to live a life true to myself, not the life others expected of me.
- I wish I didn't work so hard.
- I wish I'd had the courage to express my feelings.
- I wish I had stayed in touch with my friends.
- I wish that I had let myself be happier.

Sobering, isn't it? Sounds to me like we can sum it up fairly quickly… LIVE FEARLESSLY!!! It's all right there in front of you. The "judgments" you're experiencing are your own. I don't even get upset anymore when people to try to judge the decisions I've made. You can't take other people's opinions too personally, especially concerning an event that is beyond their level of life experience.

"Forgive them, for they know not what they do."

Living fearlessly is something you give yourself. It's derived from a deep love of "self" that others won't understand unless they too have experienced it. You don't need anyone's permission or acceptance to achieve it, only your own. Your friends, family and acquaintances may think you're mad. However, I find the idea of being restricted by the opinions of others to be far more "insane" than living fearlessly. I can think of nothing more ludicrous than allowing your life decisions to be dictated by the opinions of others.

What a completely ass-backwards way of living. That doesn't sound like "freedom" at all. That isn't living fearlessly. The ultimate expression of insecurity is to judge one's self based on the opinions of others. Fuck that shit. I'll happily continue going through my life, "failing forward" (which is also the title of an amazing book by John C. Maxwell,) rather than missing out on untold lessons, experiences and memories.

Many of you reading this right this very second are in the midst of doing something that the people around you are calling "insane." I have a message for you:

I support you.

I think you're brilliant. Even if the decision you're making is the most idiotic, dangerous, irrational decision known to mankind.

I support you.

I support your right to experience pain. I support your right to love. I support your right to live fearlessly. I support your right to make memories. I support your right to be humbled. I support your right to be poor. I support your right to dream. I support your right to not waste your life.

I might give you "advice" that's contradictory to what you want or are currently doing. However, this doesn't mean that I don't admire your courage for truly living fearlessly.

PASS THE STRESS TO THE LEFT

BITCH, DON'T KILL MY VIBE

Ascension into a dimension that's beyond comprehension for most. Igniting a fire with thoughts that aspire to transcend the struggles of life. No reason to doubt or fear going without, for faith is your most obvious friend. Keep living your life, pay no mind to the strife, for it all works out in the end.

This chapter is not about weed – not that I have anything against weed. However, much like passing a rolled up joint, the people in your life are going to pass you their stress with the same enthusiasm.

"Hey, I'm having a fucked up day… I'll call Brenden and shit all over him!"

Your friends will do it. Your family will do it. Your boss will do it. Your significant other will do it. You will do it. People love to share their stress and misery the moment it hits them. If there is one thing that can significantly distract you from your goals and purpose, it will be the negativity and stress of those around you. Avoiding this is impossible, short of becoming a hermit with no friends, family or life.

The reality is that this phenomenon of passing "energy/stress," both good and bad, is a natural occurrence in life. It's pointless to try to avoid it and attempting to do so is counterproductive. Instead, I like to do something I call "recycling energy." Most people do this naturally without realizing it. Basically, when someone is dumping on you, rather than absorbing that negative energy and then looking for someone to pass it to, you instead recycle it and pass it back as positive energy.

Recycling other people's stress takes a significant amount of patience and focus. Your natural inclination is typically to repel and or continue the "hot potato" of stress onto some other unsuspecting person.

When beginning to recycle someone's stress into a more productive form of energy, I immediately recognize what's occurring. The way I do this is by being silent. I'll let whoever is dumping their stress vent as long as they need, until I can sense that they're nearing the end of their "release."

Honestly, the key really is to stay quiet yet attentive. They may even provoke you or ask you questions. Simply reply in a calm tone and keep your answers short. Their stress and negative energy is only fed by other's energy. It doesn't matter if it's positive or negative, it will fuel their mouth diarrhea. If you don't believe me, the next time your wife/girlfriend is complaining and dumping her entire stress supply on you, try and give her practical solutions mid-conversation.

I triple dog dare your ass to try to "solve" her issue.

She'll refute every single logical solution you provide. She'll become enraged that you "think she's a goddamn moron who didn't think of that!?" and then you'll be in a fight rather than being a listener.

Pro-tip: Most women don't want you to solve their problems. They just want you to give a shit enough to listen while they complain. (Men aren't much different in this regard, though not as often.)

Our lives can be complicated, emotional and confusing endeavors, especially if you aren't playing it safe and are actually reaching for lofty goals. It's natural to absorb and create stress that you'll want to release.

After I've allowed a person to fully express themselves and unload their bullshit stress, I'll allow a moment of silence before responding, just in case there is any leftover nonsense that didn't make its way out.

"Wow, that's intense."
(That's me being empathetic.)

"I bet it feels good just to get all of that out."
(Still being empathetic.)

"If I were in that situation, I'd probably feel the same way."

Now... depending on whether I've deduced that this "stress" was in fact unjustly cast upon the person who is now attempting to unload this shit on me, or if I think they're creating their own shit storm, my answers will vary quite a bit.

If someone is simply unloading nonsense from another human being, say a family member or boss, I'll usually continue with the empathy, and they typically don't require anything more than the opportunity to vent. In that situation, I'll also make it a point to mention something like:

"Well, you've got to remember that you can't personalize someone else's issues." (This is my nice way of saying, "Hey fucker, thanks for doing to me exactly what other people are doing to you... except I'm not allowing you to fuck up my vibe.")

However, if during their blow out, I realize that this person is in fact the cause of said stress, I'll begin slowly guiding them toward taking responsibility.

"Oh wow, that really sucks. What did you do in response? Was there anything else you could have done differently?" (This is me empathizing yet beginning to move them away from blame and instead toward taking responsibility.)

Why should anyone bother doing this? The short answer is that if you don't commit to learning how to deflect other people's negative energy and how to recycle it, you'll never have any successful romances, friendships or business relationships. Can you imagine if every single time someone you cared about tried to talk to you about their fucked up day and unload their stress you responded with...

"Bitch, don't kill my vibe. I don't have time to listen to your shit today."

You wouldn't have many friends or family staying in your life for very long. Not only that, but the next time you're freaking the hell out and want to vent to someone, you're going to have a hard time finding anyone who will listen to you. They'll remember...

"Oh yeah, that fool couldn't be bothered to let me vent for two minutes, I'm not listening to his shit!"

Now I will say... it is **CRITICAL** to preserve **YOU**. If someone is unloading on you nonstop, and you're reaching a point where you simply can't handle anymore of their stress, you've got to walk away. You don't have to be rude, you don't have to be blunt, but you do need to let them know.

"Hey, I'm having a hard day as well. Can we discuss your stuff tomorrow or at the very least, later on?"

I'm speaking from experience. If I'm already under a ton of stress from other uncontrollable forces such as business, and I don't warn the person clearly about unloading their shit, I'll explode. I firmly accept that this is a part of my personality and have actually gotten quite good at managing it so it's no longer a problem. However, when I was younger and didn't really understand what was occurring, I'd blow up with the intensity of a grease fire.

Story time!!!

We'll call this story...

The time I almost beat the shit out of a Hooters girl and quit in epic fashion

The year was 2001, and I was a couple months short of my nineteenth birthday. I had moved to Florida with my best friend at the time. We were living in Daytona Beach, and our primary reason for the move was to find an adventure. We didn't really have much of a plan and had sold all of our possessions, loaded up the car and started driving from Sacramento, California.

It took us a few days to get set up, and we eventually managed to get hired at the Hooters in Daytona Beach, directly across from Daytona International Speedway.

Being eighteen years old and from a small town in Northern California, the idea of working with smoking hot "Hooters girls" all day was beyond appealing. Unfortunately, the only position that was available was a bussing position. They were short on staff and hired both me and my friend.

I had been working there for a little over two months, and I had come to learn a few things about that particular Hooters:

1) "Hot" Hooters girls don't get scheduled during day shift (except on weekends.)

71

2) Angry, old, worn out Hooters girls typically work morning shifts.

3) Morning shift Hooters girls are generally **NOT** happy that they still work at Hooters... especially if they've been there since the early nineties.

I mention the above because on this fateful day, I went toe to toe with a "legend" of that Hooters restaurant. We'll change her name to spare her the embarrassment and call her "Mary." Mary had worked at this Hooters since 1991. She was thirty-eight years old, her uniform had stopped fitting some time before Y2K, and I believe she had a bit of a drinking problem.

However, since Mary had regulars, her drunken tirades after work and terrible service were allowed to continue. (I also suspect that my sissy managers were actually afraid of this woman.) Mary stood about five feet ten inches and weighed a solid one hundred and seventy-five pounds. She had spawned a couple of kids and sort of had that "I was still serving up wings while eight months pregnant and dealing with a degenerate biker husband" kind of vibe.

The reason I mentioned Mary's "size" is that I was an eighteen-year-old, five foot nine kid, and I probably weighed in the range of one hundred and fifty-five pounds. Mary was larger, angrier and probably far more experienced in the "fighting" department.

On this day, when my stress level would exceed its maximum capacity, I had come into work and the restaurant was a disaster.

The managers had failed to mention that they were getting the wood floors re-done the night before. Therefore, every single table/chair was stacked in one room of the building. I had approximately an hour to put this entire place back together, and the chances of me getting any help from these cigarette smoking, geriatric Hooters girls was slim to none.

I worked and worked, moving quickly to return the restaurant to its original form. The harder I worked, the more angry and enraged I became as I watched these lazy ass women refill salt shakers and laugh as I rushed around them. My anger was further fueled when they would see me in the middle of doing something, and they would ask me to help them with menial tasks.

Eventually, I finished with about fifteen minutes to spare before our doors would be opening. I had worked up quite the appetite and asked one of the cooks to make a breakfast sandwich so that I could eat before my shift started.

I sat down with my food and started eating, slowly decompressing from the anger and stress of the morning. That is… until "Mary" decided to open her fat pie-hole.

"So we're busting our asses, and you're just going to sit there and eat your fucking breakfast? You're lazy as fuck, and I'm going to tell Ray (our manager) that we shouldn't have to tip you today."

I. Saw. Red.

I have no excuse for the following, I was a teenager who was stressed to the max and had had enough.

"Bitch, are you kidding me!? I've been busting my ass all morning while your fat ass has been refilling salt shakers!"

Now... in case you didn't catch the part where I fucked up and escalated things, it would be in referring to this particularly insecure, thirty-eight-year-old, muffin-topped alcoholic as a "fat ass." This statement did not go over well.

"What the fuck did you just say to me? How DARE you! I should kick your ass for saying that shit to me!"

Usually, this is the point when someone, anyone with a cooler head jumps in and begins "defusing" the atomic bomb that's about to go off... except in this case, that individual (the manager) was in the back and was unaware of the situation that was unfolding. The cooks all hated this woman's guts and were actually hoping I'd kick her in the head, and the Hooters girls are, well, Hooters girls.

"Do it, you fat, old piece of shit! I dare your busted up, leathery ass to do something. I would never fight a woman but your fat ass is close enough to that line that I'll make an exception!"

She rushed me. This woman actually came at me with all of the anger that had been building inside of that saggy, dried out, white and orange decorated body. Twenty years of slinging wings and beer to perverted men had come to a head.

"AAAAAAAAAAAHHHHHHHHH!!!!!!!" she screamed.

I moved just quick enough to avoid her and in that moment, we learned why Mary wasn't a ballerina… because the bitch had absolutely zero grace.

"POOOOOOOOOWWWWW!!!!!"

She flew face first over some bar stools. Somewhere between hitting the stools and hitting the floor, her anger managed to actually jump up a few notches, especially when she heard all of the cooks laughing hysterically. I stood there with my mouth agape. Up until that point, I hadn't been scared, but when she turned to look at me from the ground, I knew that my life was in very real danger.

At the exact moment she attempted to rush me a second time, my manager stepped between us. We continued hurling hateful words and insults at one another. My manager was laughing so hard he could barely comprehend what was happening. He dragged me off to the back office while simultaneously attempting to keep Mary at bay.

Amazingly, they didn't want to fire me. Our manager was laughing so hard, and everyone who worked there hated Mary so much that they were practically patting me on the back.

I worked that shift all day and made it a point to apologize to Mary for being hurtful and escalating things with her. I'm thinking ridiculous anger and violence were a common theme in Mary's life because she accepted my apology and then proceeded to flirt with me the rest of the afternoon. What a weirdo.

That was my last day working at Hooters. I did, however, learn that when not managed and not properly recycled, stress can lead to very negative results. I still have my setbacks in regards to being overloaded with other people's energy.

I'm a work in progress. However, applying the tips I gave above has significantly changed the dynamics of the conversations when I'm dealing with other people's stress as well as my own. I'm keener to realize when I've had enough and when I need to walk away. I've become more aware of my own "passing of stress" and am learning to drop it or let it go without having to vent to someone.

THE LOSER'S GUIDE

TO WINNING AT LIFE

Character is not built through perfection or by watching from the sidelines. It is developed at the hand of pain, adversity and failure. There is no shame in crashing and burning in life. Shame is only felt when you've been defeated and compromised your values in the process. On this day, forgive yourself, realign with your good and begin your ascension up the mountain of life.

In talking about how to un-fuck-up your life and start winning at life, I'm making the assumption that you've already done a pretty good job of epically screwing up. Perhaps you married an abusive asshole, a controlling bitch or worse, made babies with this individual. Maybe you're sick of underachieving, or you're overachieving at something that makes you want to put a bullet in your head.

If you've got a sense of discontent and regularly wake up, look in mirror and ask, "How the hell did you do this to yourself?" this is the chapter for you!

Let's start with the good news… We can fix your fucked up life, and you can start winning immediately! No matter what it is: whether you're fat, unattractive, broke, lonely, depressed, in jail – OK, I lied… I can't get you out of jail, but I can prepare you for a life once you've left the clink!

Your friends and family are going to have you believing that this stuff can't be "undone," and that you can't move past a bad marriage, dead end job, or that you'll never lose weight. They don't mean to shit on your dreams; they just don't know any better. Pay them no mind.

The only people who have a "mid-life crisis" are people who are not living a life of passion and self-expression. Most men and women will not make the necessary changes to keep growing and winning until after something horrible has happened or they're already miserable.

Rarely does anyone pre-emptively take action so they can maintain a path of growth, fulfilment and joy. You can use this chapter to get yourself back on track and start winning in your own life.

Step 1: Stop the bleeding

You're going to have one hell of a time winning at life if you keep doing dumb shit and making horrible decisions. Stop, right now. In this moment, I need you to really think about what I'm saying to you.

If you've got a date lined up with an "ex" because you're lonely, STOP. If you're stuffing your face with a Big Mac, STOP. Throw that fucking thing in the garbage before I slap the piss out of you.

Change can and does happen in the moment. It starts with a decision. You made a conscious decision to read this far, and now we're going to make a conscious decision to stop being a loser and start winning. That moment is now. RIGHT NOW!

You used to be a drug addict. You used to be an alcoholic. You used to be in a bad marriage. You used to hate your job. You used to be fat and lazy. You used to be in a passionless relationship. You used to be poor and destitute.

Whatever it is you seek to change is no longer in the present tense. As of this moment, it is now in the past. Going forward, your entire focus is on winning at the game of life.

Yes, I realize you haven't had a chance to lose the weight, kick the habits, dump the loser, start a new job, make the cash or begin winning yet. That's beside the point. We're making a mental declaration that all of the shit that makes you miserable is now a part of the past, and while your present does not yet reflect your new direction, it will very soon.

Step 2: Pick a new direction

Now is not the time to be conservative, rational or "realistic." All of that pussified thinking is what got your shit-ass life the way it is. Now is the time to nut up and start pursuing passions in life, fearlessly. Think like a boss. Think like you're already winning.

"But Brenden... I'm not a boss! I'm not winning! I've spent the last decade being a little bitch and doing what my family, friends, significant other and bosses have wanted!"

Don't worry... I did the same shit for a little while. I started out as a young adult like gangbusters. I was running a publishing company, promoting authors, booking radio and television appearances and negotiating pricing at the age of nineteen. I was on top of the world.

Then a funny thing happened. I allowed someone into my life that would bring me a ton of joy, lots of pain and ultimately assist me in losing sight of who I was. It wasn't her fault. I chose to do that and she was just along for the ride.

When I decided I'd had enough, I did not have a clear direction for how I was going to begin winning at life. I only knew that what I had been doing left me feeling empty, unfulfilled and miserable. There was nobody to blame but myself.

As you start your new journey, don't worry about the details. The details will come together as you begin this process of self-realization and passionate living.

Right now, it's critical that whatever you choose is something that stirs your soul and leaves you feeling alive. We've all had that feeling. It resides in the pit of your stomach; it accelerates your heart rate and forces a smile on your face.

THAT is joy. THAT is passion... and THAT is what life is about... THAT is winning. It doesn't matter what you do in this life as long as you never lose that experience.

If you can be dealing with the absolute shit of life and still smile at how beautiful it all is, you're doing it correctly. Bottom line... PICK A NEW DIRECTION!

Step 3: Forgive yourself

This is probably the most critical step in the entire process of going from losing to winning. Your biggest obstacle, distraction, enemy and saboteur will be your own unwillingness to forgive yourself.

That voice in the back of your head will creep in and tell you that you don't deserve to win. It will tell you that you're "hurting" other people by pursuing your passions and winning.

I have news for you. If honoring your own hopes and dreams "hurts" other people, it's because they aren't honoring their own. If they were, they wouldn't be so bothered by you stepping out of the box and taking a chance on yourself. Remember that when a man/woman is in a healthy, passionate place, the decisions and ambitions of others do not rattle them.

Forgive. Forgive. Forgive.

"But Brenden… How do I forgive myself? I've done really awful things. I let myself go, I did drugs and banged half the town!?"

It doesn't matter. Your willingness to recognize your reckless behavior and showing contrition for it is enough. Nobody expected you to be perfect. I would happily take a flawed, contrite, loving partner over someone who perceives themselves as perfect and shows little to no humility/empathy for the life around them.

The bottom line… you lived. You did a whole bunch of stupid shit and probably created some pretty bad ass memories, despite their stupidity. Fuck it! That's the point… you can't take any of this shit with you when you go, so you might as well have lived and been "big" while you were here.

Side note: Being "big" means being expansive with your life experience. It's the desire and willingness to find as many different methods of expression as you can while residing on this rock, called planet Earth.

"But Brenden… I didn't do any stupid shit. I played it safe, went to school, got a sensible degree, married a "safe" partner and had kids. Everyone thinks I'm winning… but I'm really miserable!"

I'll bet my left nut that most of the people reading this are the above. They didn't risk anything. They didn't get out and fuck up, live or create many memories.

It's not too late. I'm not saying to blow your whole life up, but you'd better figure out real quickly what it is that you want to express as a human being so that your malcontent for your own life doesn't breed into a downright resentment.

Believe me, I've been there. I did my share of dumb shit, but I also tried to play it safe. Because I wasn't able to pinpoint the source of my misery, I started to blow up everything around me. This is the equivalent of burning down your house to kill a spider under the bed.

Step 4: Have some faith

"Hey asshole, don't preach to me about your religious bullshit! I have my own beliefs!"

Don't worry... I'm not religious. I don't care what you believe, but your ass better believe in something, even if that something is yourself. If you don't have some form of faith anchoring you, you're basically a ship without a rudder. You'll keep aimlessly drifting and will be easily influenced by other faithless morons who think that faith is strictly a religious word.

Do I believe in "something" beyond us? Yes... yes I do. How the hell do you think I am able to write all of this information that is occasionally "profound?" The knowledge and ideas come from a place that I can't even begin to describe. Basically, I'll go "unconscious" while writing and it just starts flowing. After the ideas have been put down, I'll implement my personality so that it doesn't read like an esoteric biblical verse. (Believe me... I could make it sound that way if I wanted. However, I'm trying to be more relevant.)

But I digress... the point I'm trying to illustrate is that even beyond "God," "Universe," "Gaia," or whatever it is that you believe in, if anything – there is one that stands above all of the rest. I trust, believe and have faith in ME.

You're going to need to start developing the same type of relationship with YOU if you want to begin winning. Have faith that you're moving in the right direction, making sound decisions and have the ability to overcome any obstacle. Initially, you might not believe it and that's OK. Keep telling yourself that you believe, and eventually that lie will manifest itself as reality.

LOVE

THE ABSENCE OF JUDGMENT

*There is inside every man a warrior. He lies
dormant from years of negative self talk,
bad choices and keeping piss poor
acquaintances. He has forgotten his way in
this world. He has forgotten how to lead his
wife, his children and his community.*

The values and qualities of the warrior are not lost. They simply have been abandoned along with his ethics, pride and morals. He justifies it all through his "circumstance." He is too fearful to express himself or his feelings, for fear of criticism and rejection.

Remembrance for men is necessary to heal the Earth. Women want a man who loves fearlessly, laughs heartily and conducts himself with a sense of pride and purpose. He does not lie nor cheat, for these are traits of a coward. He conquers without apology... in business, in health, in love. Unleash your inner warrior today and lay claim to the fruits of being so bold.

I originally began writing this chapter on a Sunday, and on Sundays, it's important to not only give thanks for the gifts in our lives, but to acknowledge our "sins" and shortcomings.

Quite frequently, I have to acknowledge the judgment I have passed on those I've encountered in my life. Often, we pass such judgment because we believe that others should know better. What we forget is that the individual we're judging hasn't lived our life, so it's unfair to expect them to make decisions as we would.

The truth is that we're all flawed and simply make the best decisions we can based on the information we have and the knowledge gleaned from our previous experiences. Most of the time, my frustration comes from a strong desire to assist those around me in breaking the chains that bind them, be it mental, physical, spiritual or romantic.

However, I will occasionally forget that we all must experience the pain of poor decisions because that is where humility and appreciation are discovered. This applies to me as well. When I hit rock bottom in the summer of 2009, I had to write countless apology letters to the people in my life who I had turned my back on because I thought I "knew it all."

It's been quite an amazing year for me as far as "love" and "judgment" are concerned. During the summer of 2012, my ex-wife, who I was in the process of divorcing, disappeared in the middle of the night on June 21st with my four-month-old son, Phoenix. We (I) had decided to seek a divorce. I informed her of that decision three weeks prior to her disappearing. For reasons that still remain a mystery, she decided to leave with our son and left all of her worldly possessions behind.

She refused to return phone calls, text messages and emails for almost two and a half months. I was incredibly distraught and hurt. The reason I bring this up is that I wanted to share what I did during that time. I believe it is what ultimately led to the permanent reunion of me and my son, but also paved the way for the Universe to put my ex-wife on a path of growth.

I prayed for her. I extended love, positive energy and forgiveness every single night. I was well aware of her "issues" prior to deciding to enter into the relationship, and so it was unfair for me to blame her for the actions she had taken. It was not for me to judge because I was a responsible, aware human being who had decided to move forward with that union.

I still have no anger for her, regarding these actions. The first time she was forced to return him to me, I did not curse her, blame her or attack her. I smiled, grabbed my son, and gave him a big hug and kiss. I then thanked her for taking such amazing care of him.

This chapter is not about her actions, the end result or how karma paid her a severe visit less than four months later. It's about how even while going through what is arguably one of the most horrific situations a human being can endure (the disappearance of a child,) that love remains the answer.

To this day, I still love her. I love her, the way I love all of those who've played a role in the movie of my life. Whether it's business, personal, online or a simple interaction, I've done my best to extend that love everywhere I go.

I believe that love is the reason that my brutal honesty, disgusting humor and observations are received so well. Everything I say and do is anchored to love. Even in my day-to-day career as an Asset Manager, I utilize this same tact. I deal with people in what could only be classified as the "hood." I tell them the stuff that the media, counselors, politicians, parents and friends won't...

"You're fucking up your life, and I am the consequence of your fucked up life. I can help you repair your life or I can make you homeless. This will be a decision that YOU have to make."

I've made that exact statement to gangbangers, meth-heads, alcoholics, people on unemployment, you name it. It's often met with disgust and anger initially. But I keep going. I'm relentless. I look them in the eye. I speak with absolute love in my heart and in my mind, like a disappointed father.

The words are not the key to the communication. It's the willingness to be vulnerable and having the testicular fortitude to articulate the point. When you can overcome a man/woman's ego and deconstruct it through your own extension of love, you can say whatever it is you want to say, because you're no longer speaking to their "mask" but instead to their "essence" or soul.

A perfect example of this was a man named Lawrence. Lawrence had fallen behind on his rent because his priorities were broken. He was like a grown child in his interpretation of the world. Lawrence would pay his cell phone bill, buy weed and forget to pay his rent.

Lawrence was the product of a world without consequence. He did not understand what it meant to achieve or be self-sufficient. Lawrence wasn't a bad person, he just hadn't ever had anyone truly care or extend him any love.

One day prior to my evicting Lawrence, he came into my office. It's important to note that Lawrence was not a small man. He was a thirty-three-year-old, well built African-American man who stood about six feet tall and two hundred and fifteen pounds. Lawrence was accustomed to intimidating those he saw as a threat to his paradigm and was intent on doing so on this particular day.

Upon entering my office, Lawrence immediately flew into a rage because I had not given him clean rent verification for the place he was moving to.

"You motherfucker!" he shouted. "You're fucking me over, you think I'm going to let you do this to me!? This is fucking bullshit!" and on and on he went.

Finally, seeing that he was running out of profanities to hurl and threats to make, it was my turn... "Motherfucker did you bump your head on the way into my office!?"

I stood up and walked around the desk so that we were toe to toe and eye to eye.

"You owe **ME** almost two thousand dollars, and you come into my office yelling at me!? I should fuck you up right now and then have your ass arrested for assault, just on principle!"

Lawrence stood, shocked. His mouth was agape and he could not believe that this five foot nine, one hundred and ninety pound Caucasian man in a suit had just threatened to rearrange his face and send him back to prison for the "principle" of it.

He was defeated. In that moment, Lawrence had come across a will that he could not overcome. I continued... "How dare you, Lawrence. I gave you every single opportunity to succeed and to maintain a residence. You lied, you did not follow through, and you fucked me out of a lot of money."

At that moment, something far more effective than intimidation, fear or threats of violence washed over him... shame. He knew I had extended love, that I was thoroughly disappointed in him because I wanted to help him. He was embarrassed and ashamed. Lawrence had been defused and slinked out of the office without saying another word. My property manager, Terry, was astonished having witnessed the total demolition of a man and his false paradigm.

Ten days later, Lawrence approached me in the parking lot wearing a suit that was fit for a court appearance. He had just left his eviction hearing and was told he had three days to leave my property.

"I just want to apologize to you for my behavior the other day and for the way I treated you the last two months. I just left court, and they gave me and my family three days to leave. I have an interview next week for a real job, and I really can't be moved by the third day. Would you be willing to give me an extra day?" he muttered.

"Lawrence, I appreciate your apology. I'm sorry that I had to be so aggressive with you. I know you're not a bad man. I'm proud of you for apologizing and deciding to put your life back together. It's too bad that it took you becoming homeless to do it, but perhaps that is part of your path. I'll do you better than four days... take the next week to nail that job interview and pack your belongings. I only ask that you leave your keys in the drop slot when you leave."

With that, Lawrence shook my hand and thanked me for having been so fair with him. You see, Lawrence knew that I cared enough about his well-being as a man to risk him punching me in the face for my honesty. My willingness to stand toe to toe with this man while extending my love had provoked him to change.

Wherever you are Lawrence, God bless and I sincerely hope that you achieve everything you pursue in life. So with that, I would like to extend a heartfelt apology to all of you who I may have "judged" recently. Though causing you pain certainly wasn't the goal, it doesn't change the fact that it may have occurred.

I love all of you, even those I don't know. I give thanks for having you in my life in whatever capacity you occupy. Through empathy and forgiveness, it's possible that we all find our place in the clouds.

CHARACTER

WHEN OUR WORDS MATCH OUR DEEDS

If you have questions about the character of those around you, listen not to their words but rather their actions and consistency.

One of the great questions in life is, "Who can I trust?" I've pondered it throughout my life as I've had to deal with deception and letdowns. The truth is that every man or woman is flawed. The people we care about the most tend to be the ones who cut us the deepest and vice versa. As human beings, we inherently want to prevent the pain of the people we care about. We don't want to watch them struggle or get hurt.

The reality is that it's not our decision to make. As friends or loved ones, we can either choose to stand by as they make these decisions, or speak our minds and then absolve ourselves of their presence until they've sorted it out for themselves. To interfere would be to rob them of an opportunity to develop character.

Every situation is unique and often the paths people choose are ones that we're not able to accompany them down. As I go forward in my life, I realize that frequently when people ask my advice, it's not that they actually want my opinion. They simply want me to confirm that they're making a good decision and everything is going to be alright.

Well, as anyone who knows me can attest to, that's not me. It is my character to happily sacrifice my own happiness to assist a friend or family member in making a more healthy decision. I have and will continue to wear the "bad guy" hat as necessary if it means assisting someone in moving forward.

So while I cannot support every decision my friends and family make… I can say with one hundred percent love and sincerity, that things are going to be OK. My tact and grace are often lacking, but it doesn't change the fact that I say the things I do out of love.

The power of "I'm sorry" is measured by the sincerity of the actions that follow.

There is significant strength that is developed through the admission of a mistake. There is even greater and lasting character that can be gleaned from these experiences when the admission of said mistake is followed by a change in behavior.

Anyone can say "I'm sorry," just as anyone can say "I love you." However, it's the action that follows these words that makes them significant. Action will always trump words, but expressing both displays authenticity and the true character of an individual.

Authentic Game

A GUIDE TO DATING

Behind every great King is a Queen who is the rock, best friend, lover and mother that only an honorable man deserves. The true King honors his Queen with love, loyalty, sincerity and protection. There is no disunity within their relationship, only oneness and complete trust.

The Queen respects her King, never questioning his integrity or intentions. She is loved for her tender nature and willingness to be the ideal teammate. They have no room or time for childish games or cruelty. They're consumed with love and a drive to conquer all obstacles while ruling their Kingdom together.

What is authentic game? Dictionary.com defines "game" as "a competitive activity involving skill, chance, or endurance on the part of two or more persons who play according to a set of rules, usually for their own amusement or for that of spectators."

There are a few problems I see with this definition. Firstly, it's implying that there is "a set of rules." Now I don't know about you, but the people I've been "playing" with apparently didn't get the same "rules" that I received.

My rules clearly state:

No Lying – You're attempting to make a sincere connection with someone, and if you lie during this all too important "dating" stage, you risk misleading the other person about who you actually are. Honesty is critical to authentic game. If you aren't being honest during the initial dating phase, you might find yourself asking "how in the heck did I end up with this asshole!?"

Well, the reason you ended up with that person is because you were both full of shit in the beginning, and instead of you both presenting your true selves, you presented the "movie trailer" version that only emphasizes the awesome parts and leaves out all of the stuff that sucks about you. Stuff like… "I'm a chain smoking sex addict who once avoided jail time by pleading guilty to a lesser charge, and since I wasn't eighteen, I managed to keep that shit sealed; therefore, you can 'Google' my name all you want, but you're never going to find out I'm a psychopathic train wreck who's going to ruin your life and your credit!" Live. Laugh. Love.

Now I'm making jokes and am exaggerating (slightly) with the above scenario, but stuff like that does happen. I've seen it first-hand... and survived. I don't want to see any of my fellow men (or women) end up in these situations. They aren't fun and if you aren't of solid character, can really damage your outlook toward relationships.

My mom once gave me some solid advice which is, "You can't say the wrong thing to the right person." What a concept! Think about it... you can be completely unfiltered, authentic and sincere, with zero fear of the outcome. What a novel idea!

Imagine all of the time and energy you could save by being so completely yourself that others are able to make a quick decision about their level of interest.

They can either move forward in the relationship or figure out that there is no future in a matter of minutes! The moral of the story... don't be full of shit. Be authentic. Be yourself. Believe in what you have to offer. If you think she looks good, tell her. If you think she's wrong about her methods of dieting, and you in fact know for sure that consuming a large quantity of laxatives is NOT the most effect way to fit into that size 3... tell her she's wrong.

Men and women need to stop being so agreeable while on dates, unless it's sincere. I've got an incredibly sick sense of humor. Virtually nothing is off limits for me when goofing around and joking. It's quite ironic since the majority of my writings and advice center around spirituality, love and empathy, but that doesn't mean that shit isn't funny. Have you seen a duck billed platypus!? Believe me, "Universe/God" has a sense of humor.

But I digress… the point of "authentic game" is to be fearlessly you. Have some faith that the person sitting across from you will accept and be interested in the authentic version of you. If not… who cares!? That's the whole point. You're skipping through the bullshit and presenting the "truth" of who you are.

I'm a fairly charming and intelligent dude… I've pursued and been in relationships with people who I knew weren't going to be right for me. I was so wrapped up in the pursuit that I forgot to ask myself a simple question: "What happens when I actually GET her?"

Those are the messy breakup… when you have to dump someone for some shit that you already knew about them, and you disregarded as you pursued them anyway. They're going to look at you like "What the fuck, jerk? I told you I lost my little toe in a freak lawn mowing accident on our first date. But **NOW** it's a problem because it's summer and you don't want your friends to see me in sandals!?"

I've had women I began dating bring up the fact I have children well after the first date, saying they "could never be a stepmom." Wow! Thanks, probably something you could have let me know on the first date, while I was showing your ass my family pictures on Facebook.

Most relationship books and gurus recommend a shotgun approach to dating. That may work for some, but not me. I can't stand sifting through person after person who I knew I wouldn't get along with, but someone somewhere wrote that it's the "best approach," so here I am, sitting across from my fourth awful date this week.

Now, if this method works for you... kudos! Continue doing it. I, on the other hand, prefer using a sniper-like approach in addition to authentic game.

What is the "sniper approach," you may ask? I target potential mates early on. For me, a woman's character is important. I want to see what's beyond the makeup and self-tanner.

I've dated and married "beautiful" women – women who've appeared in magazine pages and on runways around the country. Blah... I want more.

The looks are a wonderful bonus, but I don't want to find myself riding in the car with you after six months, thinking, "I wonder if

I'm going slow enough for her to tuck and roll with minimal injury, so I won't have to listen to her anymore?"

I find it hilarious that men are deathly afraid of "the friend-zone." If your goal is to hook up or casually date, then yes, this isn't the place you want to find yourself. However, if you're looking for a legitimate relationship, the "friend-zone" is exactly where you want to be.

Men who can't escape the friend-zone simply don't know how to create attraction and sexual tension. The beautiful thing about the friend zone is that you're allowing someone in, and you're both being authentic – no ulterior motives or expectations.

It allows you both to decide, based on that friendship, whether they're someone you want to wake up next to for the rest of your lives. Essentially, I'm saying: start introducing yourself to and making friends with people you find attractive. That way, if you do decide they're someone you'd like to pursue later on, you don't have to worry about being attracted to them.

I love the friend-zone. Every meaningful, worthwhile relationship I've had began that way. Besides, the friend-zone ends about three inches above the female knee on the inside of the thigh.

I'm going to close this chapter with a few simple words. Be authentic. Be sincere. Be fearless and most of importantly, have fun. Men/women love to be around people who make them feel good about whom they are and the easiest way to accomplish that is by having a good, positive vibe.

Finding love is impossible because love finds you. Learn to love you, and you'll find that you become an irresistible, magnetic force for quality mates.

ONLINE DATING

THE ULTIMATE GUIDE

To sincerely love is to experience the height of human existence. It is the unifying and driving force of the Universe. However, the cultivation of lasting love is first set in motion by a willingness to be vulnerable. It is the courage to put yourself out there while being fully aware that you might get hurt, and yet you fearlessly soldier on.

The depths of love and true intimacy can only be experienced once both people have surrendered to the experience and committed to those shared values and ideals.

So you're sick of being alone, but don't want to deal with the bar scene? Your friends have told you about how they know someone who knows someone whose cousin's best friend found the love of her life on an online dating website.

Initially, you're hesitant to post your pictures for fear of the public shame that could ensue. You don't want to be judged for using online dating, and so your profile is discreet and reads more like a generic resume. It's boring as shit and nobody wants to read it.

Men, you're probably getting zero responses, and women, you seem to be attracting nothing but perverts who can't wait to send you dick pictures.

WELCOME TO THE WORLD OF ONLINE DATING!

When you signed up, you thought it was going to be better than the bar. You thought, "Yeah, this will be great! While the weirdo alcoholics are down at the pub, I'll get on here and make a real connection with my soul mate!"

Well, I've got news for you. Online dating and the bar scene are the same shit, just a different pile. That doesn't mean you can't meet the love of your life or at the very least get some consistent action from online dating. It does, however, mean you're going to have to think outside the box.

Most of what I'm going to share is geared toward men and let me tell you why. If you're a woman who's even reasonably attractive, the "key" to online dating is posting a handful of pictures, having a decent and short profile and then waiting. That's it… literally.

For men, online dating requires a significant amount of strategy. That strategy pretty much entails being completely full of shit, while sprinkling in some nuggets of truth. Now, anyone who's read my work knows that I don't condone deceit or being a liar… and that's true. However, I one hundred percent approve of this behavior when it's so over the top and funny that any rational human being would know it's a joke.

The absolute key to online dating is HUMOR. If you can be funny, you can get laid. You'll pull phone numbers from the most random women with zero effort. Don't believe me? Observe… Here is an example of my own personal "about me" section on a fairly prominent online dating website. The amount of success I get with this profile is terrifying.

'I'm a gentleman and a scholar. I once wrestled a bear in the great white tundra of Alaska. I race cars as a hobby (primarily on the street, when the other driver isn't paying attention.) I also make my own wine in the bathtub (the trick is to leave it in there while bathing.) When I'm not busy with the usual shenanigans, I enjoy a good workout (typically a thigh master or shake weight.) I'm sincere, honest, funny, intelligent and reasonably attractive. I'm that guy that you're like "hmm… he's kind of cute I guess." Then you get to know me, I make you laugh until you pee, and all of a sudden, I'm just a little bit hotter. (Also, for you ladies who are obsessed with height… YES, I'm 5'9 but I assure you those additional inches are being utilized.)

But I digress… In all sincerity I am interested in getting to know someone while dating and potentially developing something real. However, if you're just looking for an awesome person to spend time with who will make your life better…? I'm that guy. I work in real estate and develop multi-family luxury living facilities. We build big tall buildings but also do garden style stuff as well…

When I'm not at work I also write as a hobby. I'm already a published author and have my first actual "book" being released in the fall. Anything else, feel free to ask!"

As you can see, I've sprinkled in some truth, but the majority of that was nonsense. The message you want to convey while dating is that you're "light" and easy to be around. Nobody wants to read a novel about how you've been hurt in the past and are looking for "true love."

Honestly, here's what most people "want" in someone they're dating but don't have the balls to say:

- Be reasonably attractive
- Have a job
- Give me sex fairly consistently
- Don't fuck my friends

- Be fun to hang out with
- Don't beat my ass when we argue
- Don't do drugs (unless you're into drugs, then you want someone who's cool with your fucked up addictions)
- Be interesting
- Make me laugh

Doesn't seem like a whole hell of a lot to ask for!

Women, I say this with total love in my heart. If you want to attract someone other than assholes while using online dating, STOP BEING SO AGGRESSIVE ON YOUR PROFILES! I have news for you... any quality, "nice" guy who actually wants to settle down and have something real isn't going to message some woman whose profile reads like a ransom note.

"You **WILL** be over six feet tall. You **WILL** make one hundred and fifty thousand dollars per year. You **WILL** love all of my little punk ass kids as if they're your own. You **WILL** be funny, intelligent, a gentleman and you **WILL** take me on trips!"

Bitch, you **WILL** be alone forever with that fucked up attitude! Seriously, these are the women I fuck with the most through these online dating websites. I'll send some shit like

"Hey, didn't we hook up at a Christmas party in 2009? Thanks for the clap!"

The irony is that after she's done defending herself profusely against my nonsensical accusations of VD, she'll offer me her phone number.

"But Brenden, what do I put in the ideal first date section!?"

I'm glad you asked! Again, we'll take a look at mine and then collectively ask ourselves how in the hell does this shit actually work!?

"First, you would pick me up in your Bentley Convertible. You will be a model of sorts but not one of those malnourished, anorexic chicks. You will be curvy because I require a juicy ass and don't want to feel like I'll snap you in half.

After you pick me up, you'll ask me to drive so that you can nibble on my ear while I run my hand up your mini skirt. We'll go to the club and you'll start dancing with an Asian hooker named Rhonda.

You'll ask me to pay for her to come home and I'll say no. Rhonda and I will take turns doing body shots out of your ass crack before disappearing to the bathroom for some completely random and risk-ay sex.

You'll catch me mid-stroke and kick me in the balls. I'll collapse to the ground. I'll writhe in pain on the floor of a filthy piss-filled stall, weeping like a woman.

You and Rhonda will leave together and later relocate to a gay-marriage friendly state where you'll live happily ever after... thanks to me."

Or...

We could meet at a wine bar and actually get to know each other... I'm good with either option, to be honest."

There is **NO WAY** that any reasonable human being should read my profile and respond with anything other than "Dude, you're fucked. Don't ever message me again." Well, luckily for me, it seems that women are **NOT** reasonable human beings. My profile is ridiculously effective.

I'm not even that attractive. I'm not terrible looking, but I'm also not someone who's going to turn heads when he walks into the club. I am, however, funny. I am relatively intelligent, and I do my best to have proper punctuation and have a fairly extensive vocabulary. The jokes and all of that other shit are just there to draw people in... to keep them reading and hopefully, elicit a response. For men, getting the woman to respond is the hardest part.

The final ingredient to our guide to online dating is probably the most critical... the initial message. This is it, boys and girls. You've read his/her profile. You've seen their pictures. You've decided, "Yes, I would probably be seen in public with this individual."

Now it's time to reel them in. For women, this is insanely easy. Send a message that says something like: "Hi, I'm _____. How are you?" For men, it's going to take some razzle-dazzle. Men, listen up. That chick you're about to message has received thirty or forty messages... that day! You had better make your shit count if you even want her to read it.

Want an example of what **NOT** to do? Don't send anything short, don't say "hi" and don't ask "how are you today?"

"I'm terrible, fuck off! I'm a single mother using an online dating service... how the fuck do you think I'm doing!?"

Delete

Here's an example of the bullshit I'll send, and it works...

> "Smart, beautiful and seemingly sane... I can only deduce that you're on this website because you're a 21st Century Hannibal Lecter whose charms, wits and stunning glow lure in unsuspecting men... I'd be willing to not report you to the authorities, but you're really going to have to convince me. We can discuss this matter further via text and perhaps over dinner once I'm comfortable and confident I won't be your next victim.
>
> Please respond,
> Brenden"

Utter bullshit. It's a joke. The entire first message is meant to have her thinking, "What the hell am I reading? OMG! He's SOOOOO funny!" Don't believe it works? Here's an actual response I got less than 24 hours after sending the above message.

'OK, I'm not quite sure about you but your message and your profile cracked me up so I had to take a chance and message you back and try chatting! That and I haven't had a victim in a while and I'm starting to twitch, lol. "

This young woman's profile reads like this:

"Right now I own my own house and am fairly self-sufficient, so my goals would be to find someone to share my life with and continuously become more effective at my job. I have a fairly sarcastic personality and love to joke around with people that I'm close with but may hold back until I get to know you. I am very talkative and social but also very honest and open. I like country, hip-hop, and some rock, as long as it's not too hardcore rock or techno I'll be OK."

In the past I would have written her something like...

"Hey, I read your profile and you sound like a really amazing woman. It sounds like you've got your life together but know how to have fun. I'd love to hear back from you – Brenden"

And she would have ignored the fuck out of me.

But the second I accuse her of being a serial killer and offering to take her on a date with me and an Asian hooker, all of a sudden she can't **WAIT** to talk to me!

What have we learned about online dating? It makes no sense. It makes about as much sense as dating at the bar. You shouldn't take either too seriously. The most effective way to do both is to be yourself – but not the shitty, downtrodden, "my life has been rough" version of yourself.

The only way to attract someone worthwhile is by being the awesome, happy, interesting, funny version that you were before you got divorced a few times, went bankrupt, ruined your credit and crapped out some kids. Live! Laugh! Love!

NEXT

THE MOST POWERFUL WORD IN DATING

Sad but true... if you don't believe me, go ahead and "next" that player you've been tolerating and see how fast his ass comes running back. The power of "next" is that it allows you to take back your power and self-respect. It's the declaration: "If not you, then someone better."

It's not meant to be vindictive, cold or vengeful. Think of it as a verbal backhand. The true power is discovered when it's delivered with no ulterior motives, but rather a matter of fact attitude that says "your games are no longer welcome."

I see so many of my female friends asking the same question: "How do I get this guy to commit!?" The answer is to "next" his ass and see if he doesn't come running.

However, you better be really sure that you want that person coming back. In the world of dating, much like most other aspects of life, the fear of loss far outweighs the willingness to work for something good.

What I'm saying is that you pining over that person and wanting them to commit could very well be linked to the idea that you might lose them. Thus, you begin to over-emphasize their positive characteristics rather than being honest about the situation, moving on and finding someone else.

For men, it's even more complicated due to this wonderful hormone called testosterone. The male brain starts doing some funny shit when it's not getting laid regularly. You'll start justifying some of the most ridiculous, embarrassing, disrespectful behavior that your ex-girlfriend or ex-wife did just so you can get a piece of ass.

This is **NOT** healthy behavior. I've been guilty of this same idiotic behavior myself. I firmly believe that acting on such impulses is our most base function as animals and as men. Unfortunately, when you're thinking with the small brain, you can end up causing your wallet and big brain quite a bit of stress.

During the initial phase of the break-up, you're going to be extremely vulnerable. Despite the relationship's drama, the security and familiarity you shared will be something you miss. You'll deal with this longing much like a junkie does after going through withdrawals. It's not easy. Nobody ever said it would be. That's part of moving forward in life: growing, evolving, and changing into a better, well-rounded human being.

If you're willing to deal with break-ups head on rather than monkey branching like some kind of spineless, emotional basket case, you will be rewarded with a relationship in the future with someone who didn't take the easy way out, either. It will be healthy and fulfilling in all of the ways that your previous relationships were not.

Dating is going to suck for a while. You're going to initially compare every single person you date, bang or talk with to your ex. It's normal. It's not healthy, but it is normal. Don't worry, that shit will go away with time. You'll stop comparing everyone to your ex. You've got to be patient with yourself. Your brain isn't functioning properly. You'll be making all sorts of dumb ass rationalizations for the other person's behavior as well as your own, all in an attempt to justify being a pussy and getting back with them.

Don't do it. You'll regret it. He'll beat your ass again. She'll cheat on you again. They'll tear you down, and the Universe will reward your "bitch-ass-ness" with an even messier break-up and drama. I'm speaking from experience. I've been there, done that, got the child support to prove it. Temporary loneliness is not a valid excuse for contacting an ex.

You're grieving the loss of a relationship much like you would grieve the loss of someone who passed on. However, if that person kept climbing out of the local cemetery and knocking on your door, you would probably have a hard time "grieving" with a zombie at your door.

Let the relationship die. It's over. It's done. Love isn't gone forever; it's only gone on a temporary hiatus. It will return when you're ready and have done the necessary work to grow.

Stay strong, stay focused and move forward fearlessly. Let go of the past, the pain and the heartache. It no longer serves you. Once you've properly grieved, grown and healed, get back out on the dating scene and find someone who's going to be a positive force in your life.

GENDER WARS

MISGUIDED ANGER IN THE DATING WORLD

You're ready for love when you stop playing games and more importantly, don't tolerate people who still do. The amazing thing about love and meaningful relationships is that so much has to line up perfectly for a sincere connection to form. If one of you is more ready than the other, it will not work. If the timing is off by just a little bit, it won't work.

There is no more obvious sign (aside from having children) that there is a Universal Force/God that is present than when everything comes together magically, and you experience love entering your life.

This is one of the reasons that you don't need to "stress" over the wrong people, because the right ones will come into your life and be everything you've ever asked for and then some... while the wrong relationships feel more like pushing a boulder up a mountain.

If you find yourself pushing that boulder, choose to step away and allow the Universe to sort out the situation for you. Ultimately, if it's meant to be, it will be, and it won't feel forced... it'll feel natural.

Apparently, the people of this world seem to think that they're alone and having trouble dating because "the opposite sex is fucked up!" Over and over, I read women repeating to one another that "today's men are disloyal, cheating dogs." Over and over, I read about men repeating to one another that "today's women are attention-whoring sluts."

Let's clear up a few things first and foremost. Men have been "cheating dogs" for as long as they've had a set of balls between their legs. Not all men, mind you. There are quite a few who take pride in being loyal, committed husbands/boyfriends/fathers.

Likewise, women have been "attention-whoring sluts" since they discovered the effects a little bit of cleavage had on the opposite sex. Not all women, mind you. Again, there are quite a few who take pride in being classy, loyal, loving wives/girlfriends/mothers. "But Brenden, it seems like there are so many issues in today's dating world. I think you're wrong about the male/female gender's evolution."

Here's the deal: the reason it "seems" like infidelity, attention whoring and general douchebaggery are at an all time high in today's dating scene, is that we live in a world where secrets are disappearing. The internet and social media outlets are slowly removing the ability to be deceitful. The rapid exchange of news, ideas and pictures pretty much ensures that your ass is going to get caught.

However, it also makes it a very public issue. The misconception that bad behavior is on the rise is explained simply by acknowledging the fact that bad behavior is more visible than ever. The same goes for violence; with all of the bullshit news that is shown in the media, you would think we were lucky to even be surviving with all of the terror attacks, school shootings, etc.

The truth is that right now, as I am typing this statement, we're living in the most non-violent time in history. Violence as a whole is at an all-time low. Not for this decade, or the last couple of centuries – all-time. We are alive during the most peaceful time in the history of human existence. Wrap your mind around that for a moment. You probably woke up today and thought, "Oh fuck, another stressful day. When are things going to get easier?"

Human beings from every generation, since the beginning of time, would HAPPILY switch places with you to have the opportunity to avoid dying of an infected wound, a dinosaur chewing their faces off (yes, I know humans and dinosaurs didn't exist at the same time... it's a joke,) and the ability to pick berries without being kidnapped and raped by a nearby tribe.

Now, let's get a little bit personal. Your "issues" in dating aren't the opposite sex. They're you. The emphasis that human beings have placed on ensuring that they aren't alone is absolutely ridiculous.

God forbid anyone be discerning when dating. I thoroughly believe that the over-emphasis on "being in a relationship" is simply the product of people who are leading unfulfilling lives.

Women are notorious for starting relationships with men simply because they don't have any other hobbies. They make a man their hobby. I have a feeling that this is why many women are dating abusive, disloyal pricks. It gives them a challenge and something to "do" with their otherwise pointless existence. Rather than taking on more ambitious goals and worthwhile endeavors, they take on players and douchebags under the guise of love.

I know we've all had those female friends who monkey branch from jerk to jerk and almost immediately begin complaining about the new guy.

Here's a free pro-tip: If you're complaining about the new guy/girl you're dating within the first ninety days, it's not going to work... ever. You might be able to milk that sorry ass relationship for a few years or perhaps you're really stubborn and will stick it out, but you should always know you're forcing a round peg into a square hole. Please spare the rest of us and don't complain later when your relationship is mired in drama.

Now before I go alienating all of my amazing female readers, let's discuss why men do the stupid shit that they do. Men "cheat" for a number of reasons. However, I'm not really going to delve into that particular topic, specifically. What I want to discuss is the idea that men seem to think that they're a slave to the desires of their dicks.

Young men are constantly on the prowl for sex. Generally, this is the first and last thought they have every single time they wake up. Most men will use it as a cop out for incredibly stupid decisions they make, such as cheating. "Oh baby, I couldn't help it. I just was really horny and you weren't giving it up often enough."

Look, I'll put my testosterone levels and desires for sex against any man. I've been that guy up above (minus the cheating part.)

However, I outgrew it. I still have the same drive/desire, but I've found a deeper purpose in life than chasing ass and thus have a more balanced existence.

Men act like dogs because they don't have anything else to fill their time. Most men will avoid "self-evaluation" and instead will seek an ego boost in the form of sexual deviancy. They misbehave and chase because somehow this validates their existence and gives them a sense of purpose. It's bullshit.

This isn't to say that you shouldn't pursue women you're interested in or have sex. Hell, I'm a firm believer in having a healthy sex life and enjoying the female form. However, when you've begun straying from your goals, ambitions and integrity in the pursuit of pussy... you're doing it wrong.

If you're risking losing a faithful wife, embarrassing your family and shaming yourself for the sole purpose of sex, it's time to re-evaluate your life.

The sex is the expression of unfulfilled desires, and for the most part, they're largely not going to be related to the act of sex. (That's not to say there aren't instances that it really is about sex due to a lack of intimacy in the relationship, but that's a whole other topic.)

"But Brenden, what is the solution, how do I stop having these experiences in dating?"

Simple… you commit to finding your purpose. Firmly establish the role of dating in your life and begin disciplining yourself to allow people to come and go from your life effortlessly.

For the most part, men and women will give you plenty of red flags. Often, men and women fight to preserve dysfunctional relationships. They have no reason other than a fear of the unknown or of being alone.

Absolutely nowhere is it written that you must "play the game" when it comes to dating. Nobody is forcing you to tolerate bullshit from either gender. Fearlessly open up, see how the other person handles it and if it doesn't "feel" right, move on.

"Brenden, you're single… how is dating going for you?"

I'd say it's going fabulously. I'm in love with me and because of that, I don't need to seek validation from the opposite sex. I simply pursue my goals, dreams and passions and allow women to enter my life and exit it without much "angst." I don't fight for anyone, anymore. To me, it seems like such a juvenile endeavor. I value my time and peace of mind too much to spend it in unhealthy, co-dependent relationships.

The ultimate irony is that my disposition and "lightness" toward love and dating has resulted in me magnetizing incredible women into my life. It doesn't mean they all stay, and for various reasons.

I'm not going to force/coerce/manipulate anyone to be in my life. Fuck that shit. Been there, done that, wasted a decade learning why it's pointless.

Dating, to me, means getting to know someone without ulterior motives. I go into every interaction with the intent of seeing what she's about and whether she is someone with whom I would like to continue spending time. The people who are meant to be in your life have a certain "stickiness" to them and will continue to hang around.

Bad "love" is **NOT** better than no "love" when it comes to dating. The greatest gift you can give yourself is the self-love necessary to forgive and to be completely authentic and vulnerable, yet remain so committed to your convictions that you're unmoved when others attack or attempt to hurt you.

Rather than occupying your time with dating and wondering why you're alone, begin pursuing passions. Find as many different methods to creatively express yourself as possible. Learn a language or how to play a musical instrument. Take a dance class, write, paint, travel, exercise. Love and healthy relationships will find you when you're in a place of harmony and are comfortable with your own "being." This isn't something you have to stress about or over-analyze.

Loyalty

THE MOST MISUSED WORD IN RELATIONSHIPS

My loyalty is to a set of principles and values... not people.

You ever have those times in your life where you can tell that things are changing dramatically and your entire existence is about to be redirected? I fucking LOVE that feeling. Most people shit their pants when dealing with those types of gut instincts or "changes." That's my sweet spot! I swear to God, if any of you ever go through "shit is hitting the fan" mode, I'm the guy you want to talk to. Pressure is my middle name! (OK, I lied: it's actually Michael.)

As the winds of change are blowing, I'd like to delve into a topic that I believe is rarely ever discussed without a misuse of the word – loyalty. Typically, these are the quotes we see associated with it...

> "If they stand by you during the bad times, they deserve to be there during the good times."

Wrong. What if when the good times arrive, they've changed so dramatically that they no longer encompass the values that you honor?

> "A woman's loyalty is tested when her man has nothing... a man's loyalty is tested when he has everything..."

What? I've been with women when I had "nothing," and they stood by me... this is true. However, they also made my life a living hell to the point that their loyalty wasn't worth shit. It would have been easier without their "loyalty."

What is the obsession with "loyalty?" Most of the time, the words loyalty and unconditional love are used interchangeably, but they really aren't the same thing. I think this chapter/rant will make much more sense if perhaps I explain the differences between the two in my own words.

My personal "code," if you will, is this: I am loyal to a set of values and principles. They're based on honesty, trust, positivity, sincerity, authenticity, reliability, empathy and ethics. The people in my life, whether they've been there for a week, a day, or years, all receive my loyalty based on their expression of these values.

However, if you violate my code, you are dishonest to the point of being vile. If you cheat, scheme and ignore the values that I hold dear, you instantly lose my loyalty. It doesn't matter if you're my family, friend, wife, girlfriend, or even my kids.

This does NOT mean that I don't "love you." This does NOT mean that I don't accept you and forgive you. This does NOT mean I won't be your friend and advise you. It does, however, mean that I will hold you accountable. It means that I will not defend your shitty behavior. I am and have been the inconvenient truth more than a few times for those closest to me.

Some understand it, while others believe it to be disingenuous or disloyal. For me, that is not the case. I hold you accountable because I care. I do not waver because I love you. I refuse to defend or accept your behavior because I'm trying to assist in guiding you toward authenticity. I fully anticipate and accept to be held to similar standards or codes of conduct. If I violate my own "code," I am prepared to be called out on that hypocrisy and am not going to blame anyone for doing so.

Here is a question for all the ladies. All I ask is that you be one hundred percent honest with yourselves when answering. You know that guy you've been with all of these years? You know the guy you've "stood by through everything," and "took back when he was wrong?" Did you do it because you were loyal to him, or was it because you were terrified of being alone and didn't want to deal with the repercussions of holding him accountable?

Even now, I can sense the unease by just having asked the question. We're going deeper right now, and if we ever hope to make any significant progress as a species, certain "accepted truths" are going to have to be questioned. Some of you will say, "I stayed loyal because I love him and could not live without him in my life!"

That's fine.

It sure sounds good to say and to read, doesn't it? Here's the problem: what does loving him and staying in his life have to do with holding him accountable for terrible behavior? Do you live with principles or a code? Perhaps his shortcomings as a human being somehow justify your own; therefore, if you stay with someone like that, you'll never have to be responsible for your own personal growth.

Now we're getting somewhere. In my estimation, there are very large numbers of women and men walking around touting "loyalty" as their reason for staying in fucked up relationships. In reality, the reasons are co-dependency and fear. But it's just not "cool" to say…

> "Yeah, Brian and I are still together. I've stuck with him through everything. It feels really good to have someone around more fucked up than I am so that I can keep being a piece of shit and never have to stress about growing or evolving as a person."

Hello, co-dependency. Live. Laugh. Love!

"Loyalty" and "true love" are going to vary from person to person. I am simply offering you an explanation of what I've observed and how I interpret it. This topic is sure to piss off a few people who are now staring squarely down the barrels of their own truths. Or maybe you're deeply offended by my assertions and think I'm talking out of my ass (which is certainly possible… bear with me, I'm still learning as well.)

Then again, maybe I'm wrong. Maybe there is a profound connection that is forged by wilfully compromising your own integrity to stay loyal to a man/woman.

I am still at what I would call the "beginning" of my life, and so I cannot claim to know what the middle or end look like. I know that I believe in love, friendships and unity. I know that I base them all on sincerity, honesty, empathy and forgiveness. For the life of me, I just can't imagine living an entire life without accountability or without compassion.

In my mind, holding those you care about most accountable is how you say, "I love you so much that I'm willing to lose you if it means you're a better person for it."

I feel the same way about my writing. If the inconvenient truths that I share rub you so far the wrong way that you never come back, yet you are even slightly more enlightened or a happier person, I'll take it.

That's a victory for me and you. Fuck my book, fuck my opinions and fuck my honesty. I don't want the "credit" for being the one who forced you to potentially "expand" or "grow." Frankly, I don't need the assurance and neither does my ego. All I care about is that you're living a joyful, fearless and passionate existence.

THE NUCLEAR OPTION

WHEN LOGIC TAKES
A BACKSEAT TO EMOTION

Your creativity, self expression and passion are your gifts to the world. However, it's up to you to have the willingness to honor them and the courage to pursue those desires. Let your light shine fearlessly and never forget who you are no matter how much the world tries to convince you otherwise.

I'm not a political writer… and thank God, too! I actually tried to write a little something about the "nuclear crisis in North Korea," but my subconscious mind wouldn't allow me to comment on such douchebaggery. Instead, we're going to take the current political shit storm and apply it to other more relevant aspects of life… in particular, relationships. I've had more than a few women I've dated or been involved with try to pull this stunt to get their way.

I'm sure that men pull this same dumbass stunt, but unfortunately my experience is limited to women in regards to dating. What is "the nuclear option" in a relationship? My definition is when someone threatens to "end things" because of minor disagreements or differences of opinion.

I had one particularly "special" woman who would regularly bust out the nuclear option to manipulate me into doing what she wanted. As I got older, I recognized the tactic and stopped tolerating it. The hilarious part is that there hasn't been a woman since who understands why I happily end things with them, often times abruptly when they go "full potato" and start telling me, "Fuck you! I'm going to leave if you don't do XYZ!"

My typical response is, "Aww… you didn't get the memo. I'm not a man you can EVER pull the nuclear option with. Now pack your shit, Skippy, because your time is done." The amount of out-of-context, pseudo "female empowerment" quotes from Marilyn Monroe that circulate the internet isn't helping either.

Women see shit like… "I'm selfish, impatient and a little insecure. I make mistakes, I am out of control and at times hard to handle. But if you can't handle me at my worst, then you sure as hell don't deserve me at my best."— Marilyn Monroe

What in the actual fuck? How is this in any way, shape or form "inspiring?" This might be one of the dumbest goddamn quotes I've ever read. Newsflash! Marilyn Monroe at her "worst" was a pill popping, alcoholic whore who was fucking single men, married men and anything in between.

What man should tolerate that kind of fucked up behavior so that he can "deserve her at her best?" Her "bests" were by all accounts fleeting and few and far between. Yet on my Instagram, Facebook and Twitter, this dipshit movie actress is being lauded as some sort of "women's empowerment icon." Get out of here with that shit! You know who a "women's icon" is!?

Oprah Winfrey?

How about Marie Curie?

Better yet… why not Lisa Kitter?

OK… I'm slightly biased since that last one is my own mother, but still.

Hopefully, you're beginning to see my point: misguided individuals are using the threat of "taking away love" (the nuclear option) as a means to manipulate their partners. I'm fully aware that I'm probably going to piss off some women with these words.

As I said, I've never dated dudes, so I can't air my grievances about men applying the "nuclear option" to relationships. If you're dating a dude who does use it to get his way, you're dating a bitch.

Men don't make threats, bitch-ass men do. Men give warnings. Threats are hollow and weak.

Warnings are sincere and have every intention of being followed through on. My "ex" finally used the nuclear option one last time, and our conversation unfolded something like this...

While looking deeply into her eyes and kneeling before her on our bed, I began:

"You realize that this is a defining moment in your life. This moment will change the trajectory of many lives including our daughters. You cannot have this moment back, as I have warned you that if you ever threatened me with this again, I would absolutely leave and never come back. Do you understand what I'm saying to you?"

"Yes. I understand."

"Good. I'll be out in thirty days."

Within hours of this conversation and for the following months, she begged me to not leave, pleaded with me to come back, and insisted that "I made a mistake." Exactly one month later, I moved out and that was that. After six years, two children, three houses and hours of time together, it was over. Eventually, you're going to crap out if you gamble long enough, and on that particular day, she rolled snake eyes.

My point is that nobody, man nor woman, deserves to be manipulated with constant threats of "breaking up" or "withholding love." It's a coward's move, and using the nuclear option only breeds resentment and negativity.

If you're in a co-dependent relationship that regularly experiences extreme swings from "good to bad," and the nuclear option is a common occurrence, I would strongly suggest you vacate that toxic situation.

It will not get better, and for every such situation that does improve, I'll show you hundreds that escalate to violence and other embarrassing displays of human behavior.

Have some class, leave with your dignity and do not tolerate anyone who pulls this shit.

To trust or not to trust... that is the question.

Trust... one word that can make or break relationships of all kinds. Whether it is business, romance, family, or friendship, trust is essentially a way of measuring your faith in another human being. I could take this topic in a variety of directions in regards to trust. However, we're going to speak a little more specifically on the actual application of putting trust into those around you.

This won't be about "universal trust," "God," or "faith" in an esoteric sense. Instead, I'd like to discuss trust in the more functional meaning of the word.

Conventional wisdom says that "trust is earned" over time and that when initially forming any type of relationship, that we remain guarded until the individuals involved feel as if the other person has "earned" the right to be trusted. Personally, I've never operated that way. It feels foreign and unnatural to remain fearful or distrusting of those around me. I believe that there are consequences to either approach and pros to them as well.

I relish the opportunity to put my faith and trust in another as frequently as possible. I firmly believe that doing so allows the "truth" to bubble to the surface faster. I'll be honest though; doing this WILL cause you to get "hurt" more frequently. It's normal to experience pain when allowing people in, especially because most of the world doesn't think this way (at least not that I'm aware of.)

Hell, most people are going to be confused at your willingness to open up and trust them so quickly, and they will probably fuck it up out of unfamiliarity alone.

I'm sitting here thinking (which is never a good thing, because I usually just let the writing flow,) and the only way I can describe my approach to trust would be the "digging your own grave" analogy.

Basically, I'll hand you the shovel and give you one hundred percent of my trust and respect. As we begin our relationship (in whatever capacity,) I'll pay attention and remember everything you say and do. I'm not looking for anything, but I try to be as present as possible in my day to day interactions, especially with new people. Thus, I tend to remember statements, stories and general facts/conversations that I have.

As the days and weeks go by, the individuals will do one of two things: they will begin slowly digging the grave with lies, deceptions, half truths or lack of follow through, or they'll maintain my trust by being consistent. Unfortunately (especially in the world of dating,) I've noticed that because of my sincerity and consistency, most of these women start digging that fucking hole a hell of a lot faster than necessary. It's as if they're aware that I'm undressing their soul and start to panic.

Once they've dug that grave deep enough, I kick them in that motherfucker and delete them from my life.

Is this the correct approach? I'm not sure. My gut tells me that it is, because I have no desire in wasting time on superficial relationships of any kind. I don't want a relationship that is based on our mutual love of being full of shit. I'd rather stay at home and talk to my Rottweiler than deal with that nonsense.

At the end of the day, I, just like you, have to do what feels correct for ME. I feel that if I've given adequate opportunities and set realistic expectations, then it's up to the individuals in my life to either reciprocate sincerely or to fuck off.

GROWN FOLK TALK

THE BITCH SLAP YOU NEED TO MOVE FORWARD IN LIFE

I'm feeling like quite the cheeky bastard today, so I'm thinking we'll discuss some difficult life subjects with a sense of honesty and candor that can only be provided while residing safely in the "trust tree." With this chapter, I hope to provoke some thought on subjects that are normally handled with "kiddie" gloves.

As I write this, cheating season is upon us. For whatever reason, it has always seemed that many people lose all sense of morality from mid-May through September.

Every summer, I'm inundated with the same impossible questions, such as...

"I think she's cheating on me, what should I do, bro?" or "We're fighting constantly, and he won't have sex with me anymore... what should I do?"

To the first question... dump her. To the second question... dump him. I'm not sure what the infatuation is with "making it work," but that might just be the stupidest excuse for people choosing to remain in co-dependent relationships that I've ever seen.

I'm serious... if you believe your partner is cheating on you and the trust is gone, why would you stay? Don't say, "Because I love him," because that's bullshit. You're just too cowardly to deal with the reality that lies on the other side of making a decision. Trust is the bedrock of any relationship. When you stay in a relationship after the trust has been compromised, you're simply delaying the inevitable because you're a pussy.

"But Brenden... we're married, we have a house, children and a life together!"

So what?

What exactly does any of that have to do with anything? The trust is gone. Aside from kids together, you have NOTHING left. Zilch. As John Mayer would say, "You're slow dancing in a burning room." I can completely empathize with the hesitation and fear associated when leaving someone with whom you share children.

Believe me... I get it. I did it twice, and both times were terrifying. However, fear is not a reason to stay in an unhealthy relationship. If you're reading this and are in a relationship where the trust has been compromised, do yourself and your partner a favor and start planning your exit.

For those of you who have issues with a lack of trust, a lack of sex, constant fighting, discontent, violence or loss of attraction within your current relationship, and who DON'T have children...

How in the hell are you going to tolerate baby momma/baby daddy drama, and y'all don't even have any babies!!!????

Man... maybe I'm just a huge asshole, but why in God's name would you tolerate such bullshit from someone with whom you have no "lasting" ties? I see both men and women fighting, struggling, arguing, battling and crying over these relationships. They love to dress them up as some earth shattering "love" rather than cop to the reality that it's a co-dependent relationship and brings out the worst in both people. Live! Laugh! Love!

Your life is short. Let me repeat that. Your life is short. You have no clue when this ride will end. I was having a really good conversation with a friend yesterday, and I was explaining this exact point to her. I don't want to spend my time complaining, whining and trying to "change" someone who was probably perfectly awesome before I came along, simply because I want the relationship to "work."

Do ANY of us really need more "work" in our lives? Take two steps back from the relationship, get honest with yourself about why you're in it, and then stop getting pissed off at someone for being exactly who they were when you got together. Men and women are both guilty of waiting for the other person to change.

Knock that shit off. That person – with the right person – is perfectly capable of love, loyalty, passion, kindness and romance. Have you ever stopped to think that perhaps YOU are not that "right person," and thus it's impossible for that person to express those qualities?

I know I've been in situations and relationships that had turned toxic, and I found myself thinking, "Geeze… I don't ever remember being this much of an impatient asshole before." That's because I'm NOT! I had simply allowed myself to stay in a situation that had turned unhealthy and didn't vacate it in time.

Lesson learned... never again.

Now before you go dumping your significant other and proceeding to murder a tub of ice cream after cutting yourself, there is a silver lining.

There is in fact "someone" out there that will make the relationships "easy" for you. I know these relationships exist for a couple reasons. One, because I myself have had one, though fleeting. Two, I personally know couples who are madly in love and emit a beautiful aura when in one another's presence. "True love" isn't bullshit. It's real.

"But Brenden... what does it take to experience it?"

It takes you being willing to spend some time alone. It takes you actively growing, acknowledging and changing your own shitty qualities. It takes a significant amount of patience and faith that the Universe will in fact deliver to you the right person, at the right time.

He/she is out there. They're probably wondering the same thing you are: "Where the hell is this mythical person?" Every single day, I observe couples who didn't have the patience and instead decided to enter into serious relationships with the "rebound" guy/girl. Good luck with that shit! Again... been there, done that, got the son to prove it.

There are certain aspects of life where shortcuts are NOT an option, and this is one of them. I once read that for every year spent in a serious relationship/marriage that has ended, you should take 3-6 months to be alone. Now as you all know, I'm not big on "rules" or arbitrary guidelines, but this one does yield a valid point.

We're all aware that if ANY of us really wanted to get into a "serious relationship," we could probably do it in a matter of days. Of course, I could also score some heroin fairly easily, but that doesn't mean it's a good idea.

Monkey branching from relationship to relationship is unhealthy, destructive and a massive character flaw. It's not a matter of IF that new relationship will end, it's a matter of WHEN... and when it does, that other person is going to be PISSED.

I'm not preaching this shit from an ivory tower. I'm speaking from real life experience. "Love" was my addiction, and I was damn good at it. Romance, love, passion and all of that mushy shit is my specialty.

Thankfully, I realized just because I "can" sweep a woman off of her feet doesn't mean I "should." I'm at a place now that is patient, content and much more mature. (Well, aside from my humor of course.)

I know that I sometimes write in a harsh manner that can be a bit hard to swallow, but my intention is ALWAYS to assist you in leading better, happier and more productive lives. When we all realize our own personal power, the world can shift in a matter of days.

MASTERING
FORGIVENESS

AND TAKING BACK YOUR POWER

Authenticity, self-acceptance and self love go far beyond just dating. Whether you're concerned with dating, business relationships or friendships, people aren't going to be drawn to you if YOU aren't excited about you. Part of being a happy, healthy human being means accepting that you're flawed and that you will make mistakes.

In previous chapters, I've touched a bit on the need to be authentic and be yourself if you wish to attract quality, compatible people into your life.

The question that naturally arises when telling someone that they need to be themselves or accept themselves is: "What if I don't like 'ME'? Where do I go from there?"

The common thought process is:

"I know I'm SUPPOSED to love myself, but I've done some really fucked up shit. How the hell do I get over that?"

Or...

"But my entire life, people have been telling me that I'm ugly, stupid and fat. They're right, I am ugly, and I have been fat since I was kid. Hell, even my own mom thinks I'm worthless!"

These are certainly valid questions, and we're going to tackle them right now. This will be somewhat heavy duty.

If you are just looking to get laid and have no desire to become a better person, you might want to skip this chapter: I don't want to bore you. If, however, you're trying to grow as a person, and you've got some serious and more ambitious goals – relationship wise or even just interaction wise in your everyday life – then this will be right up your alley.

The thing that we have to talk about is **FORGIVENESS**. It's probably the number one thing, as a man, that has helped me to not only overcome the really fucked up decisions I've made, but also assisted me in having a healthy relationship with my past and being able to put my past into a proper context.

A lot of you, both men and women, have a tendency to beat yourselves up over whatever you've done in your past, and you think your story makes you who you are. It kind of tells a bit, but not really. Your past only holds as much weight as you give it.

Whether your goals are in fitness, relationships, or otherwise, forgiveness should absolutely be your number one priority.

You're not perfect. You're never going to be perfect. You're going to fuck up repeatedly.

Between now and the time that you've finished reading this chapter, you will likely have some negative thoughts about yourself – that is one form of "making a mistake." You better learn to let go of that shit and be able to forgive yourself for not being one hundred percent on your game all of the time.

Let's talk about forgiveness. When you came to this planet, you arrived looking like a brand new, crisp, clean, white sheet of paper. You had no flaws, no wrinkles, no stains; you were nice and clean.

You were perfect…

Until you got yelled at, because you did something you weren't supposed to at age three. Then at age eight, you asked your first little girlfriend out, and she laughed at you. Oops.

Maybe at age twelve, you started to mature, you put on a little bit of weight, and kids started teasing you. Fast forward to age fourteen; you tried out for sports, and you sucked. Then that one kid wanted to kick your ass.

In high school, you asked out another girl, and she rejected you, humiliating you in front of everyone. Maybe you finally got your first boyfriend, and he slept with you and dumped you. Then he told everyone you were a slut.

You went to college. Dropped out, couldn't hack it. You got your first job, and you got fired because you had no skills. Then you monkey branched onto a dude who got you pregnant and left you.

And now, you're sitting there like a wadded up ball of paper… you're crumpled up, creased up, you're scarred up, and shit is just not right. You have no context, no idea who you are, no idea where you were, and you just know that people have been beating you down your entire life.

Well… FUCK EM'!

Alright, first thing we're going to do: you're going to write some letters.

This was something I did when I was eighteen. I didn't have the best relationship with my dad growing up. We have a phenomenal relationship now, thank God, but we didn't always. Because of that, I had some challenges with anger when I was younger. I wasn't a warm person when I was a kid, wasn't really warm in high school. I always had plenty of friends, but I was kind of known for being brutally honest and a little bit of an asshole.

I didn't want to be like that anymore. So when I was eighteen, I wrote letters.

First, I wrote a letter to everyone I ever thought hurt me — I mean EVERYBODY — and I was forgiving them.

> "I forgive you for making fun of my clothes when I was in eighth grade, and I was super poor. I forgive you for teasing me about being short when I was a freshman in high school. I forgive you dad, for calling me names and making me feel like shit about myself when I was a kid. I forgive you, mom, for spoiling me and my having to learn a sense of hard work later in life."

Whatever I could think of, I forgave these people. I wrote it all down.

This exercise should take you more than a few minutes. It's somewhat emotional. Mine weren't too heavy, but there are people with far worse backgrounds and childhoods than I could ever imagine, for whom this might be a much more emotional process. The point is that I did the exercise. I sat down, I wrote it all out, and I forgave all of them.

Forgiveness is your only way of taking back your power.

If you are under the age of eighteen, you're still a kid, and you get to be a victim. It sucks, and I'm sorry. Life is not fair, and it really sucks that people are doing horrible shit to you. If you're over the age of eighteen, you're an adult now. We don't get to be victims anymore.

You are not a victim anymore.

You're an adult, so now you get to be responsible. The way you start that process is by having a healthy relationship with the past. A healthy relationship with your past comes by taking the power away from all of the people who have ever shit on you. You do this by forgiving them. Forgiveness is the only way.

"But Brenden, I don't want to forgive them! I HATE them! Those bastards ruined my life, they don't deserve forgiveness!"

Being pissed off at them for the remainder of your days isn't going to hurt them. Most of the people who have hurt you don't know that you're angry at them, and they most likely wouldn't care even if they did. They've got their own shit to deal with. Your anger or hatred isn't affecting them; YOU are carrying it around, and it is becoming toxic in YOUR life. It isn't holding them back; it's keeping YOU stuck and not allowing YOU to move forward.

I see a lot of young dudes and a lot of women who just can't let that shit go. You've got a lot of anger inside of you that is just balled up, it's tearing you apart, and you have no idea how to deal with it. I'm telling you right now: the only way to deal with it is to forgive.

You are going to write that letter. You can write individual letters, you can write one to mom and dad, one to your little girlfriend, one to your kid sister, whoever… or you can do it all in one letter. It doesn't matter; the point is to get it out of you. Get all of that shit out of you. It is imperative that you get it out.

Once you've written your letter, burn it. Fucking BURN IT. Write the whole thing, cry all over that paper if you need to, and then burn it.

With your next letter, you're going to be forgiving yourself. This is going to be the hard one. This is the one where you're really going to want to cry. If this doesn't make you cry, you're not trying hard enough. It is heavy duty.

> "I forgive you for not being perfect. I forgive you for putting on weight in college. I forgive you for not saying the right things to girls. I forgive you for embarrassing me. I forgive you for not being more athletic."

Forgive yourself for whatever you can think of – anything and everything that you feel guilty for, shame about, your regrets, whatever. All that shit that you're insecure about, anything you think is "all your fault," write it down.

I've met a lot of people who feel like the world is horrible because they're in it. It's not. It just is, and you can't take this shit too seriously.

Stop blaming yourself for everything and allowing guilt and shame to fester inside of you; that's too heavy a burden to carry with you through life.

Write it out... forgive yourself. You've got to. It takes time. That letter, to myself, was the most emotional for me.

This exercise is basically ground zero for you as a human being. If you want to rebuild your psyche and self-esteem and actually have a positive, healthy approach to life, this is how you do it.

You write the letter(s) forgiving everyone who has ever fucked you over, and you take your power back from them. Then you write the letter to yourself, about everything you've ever screwed up on – ever – and you take the power back from that little voice that's inside your head that keeps saying you're not good enough, or you're not special... all of that negative shit. You take all that power back by forgiving and letting it go.

Keep writing until you can't think of anything else. Then when you're done writing, you burn that one too.

OK, now we've burned our letters.

Next, every morning and every night, you look in the mirror, and you say, "I love you." You look straight into your own eyes. If you are uncomfortable doing that, it means you need to keep practicing.

"I love you. I appreciate you. You're amazing. I love this, this and this about you."

You repeat that, every morning when you wake up and every night before bed. It takes 2 to 3 minutes, and you do it until you can look yourself in the eye without looking away. That's the goal.

You are not your mind. You are not your insecurities. You are not your emotions. I know everyone seems to think that – you're not, you can't personalize this shit. Some of this negativity is an automatic response to the outside world, and some of it is just old crap you haven't dealt with yet.

I'm trying to teach you how to deal with it today, because unless you do, you're going to go forward in life and perpetuate the same exact life experiences over and over again.

I know this, because in my twenties, I did the same shit. Time and time again, I kept having the same type of issues and had to do the same exercises. There is no shame in doing this.

Learning to forgive yourself is like laying the foundation when building a house. It is critical. If you don't do this now, your house is going to come crashing down on top of you later in life. I guarantee it. You can't move forward in life until you've got a proper context for the past and are completely at peace with it.

Forgiveness isn't just about old stuff or long-term mistakes either. I practice forgiveness with "ME" daily. Every single day, I have to forgive myself for things I do, for thoughts I have, for insecurities I'll come up with "in the moment."

The difference between me and the average person is that I deal with my mistakes and insecurities in that moment; I don't let them fester and build into something larger that will eventually crush me. Left unaddressed, this is what ultimately ends up happening to most people.

The inability to forgive yourself and forgive your insecurities allows those insecurities to pile up and expand; they create an emotional wall around you. You eventually become emotionally unavailable and generally, full of shit. Then you're average, and nobody wants to wake up one morning and be average. So you combat this by forgiving yourself every single day.

Another thing I see a lot, particularly with men, is regret or uncertainty about opening up to people – particularly to women they're interested in or involved with. I'm telling you right now: you don't ever have to apologize for opening up and sharing yourself with someone. It takes balls to open up.

I get a lot of questions like:

"I talked to this girl I really like, and she shot me down. Did I do something wrong?"

No, you didn't do anything wrong. When you get shot down, it says more about the other person than it does about you... especially if you're coming from a legitimate, authentic place. If you're opening up because you're whiney and you have co-dependency issues, that's obviously different.

If you actually like a woman (or a man), and you express yourself in a sincere and honest way – in a very adult, healthy, emotional way – you have nothing to be ashamed of. That takes balls. If anything, you should be patting yourself on the back. It's not easy. It's total bullshit to say it's "beta" or "weak" to share how you're feeling. That's fucking stupid.

If you're just trying to get laid, all you have to do is zero in on emotionally insecure women, treat them like shit, and they'll come flocking – which is horrible, but if that's your only goal, that's how you do it. However, if you're actually healthy, and you want a real relationship with someone... and you're concerned that you're being too "emotionally available," that's bullshit. You're fine. The right person is going to recognize your sincerity and respond.

I wanted to share this because I got rejected recently by someone I was interested in. I shared my feelings, and she didn't feel the same. I got more out of being rejected outright than if I'd kept my feelings to myself. What kills me is the ambiguous part, where you don't know how the other person is feeling.

When someone is indirect, that shit pisses me off. When someone is direct and just says, "Hey, I'm flat out not feeling you," that's cool. Check that little box off the sheet; you're done. You get to move on. Instantly, in that moment, your feelings stop.

One of the best pieces of advice I ever received is that the value you place on the person you're pursuing should be in direct proportion to how much they value you. If they don't value you, then they should cease having value to you. If they don't recognize your value, there's ultimately nothing there. That applies not only to romantic relationships, but friendships as well.

When people value your time, value your life force, value your energy and your presence, they make an effort to let you know that and to be around you. They make the effort to learn from you and experience you. In return, you get to perpetuate that cycle and do the same thing for them. However, if you have people in your life who don't value you, and you are overvaluing, that's OK, but you have to catch yourself.

I'm guilty of overvaluing individuals as well; I've done so recently. It happens to the best of us. You just have to catch it, and then remind yourself that you are worthy of good feelings and reciprocity. Everything you're putting out there that is positive, like the sincere compliments that you give to a man or a woman, is absolutely deserved in return.

A lot of people start running into issues with reciprocity and value when they stop being sincere. Men, especially, tend to implement all of these stupid dating rules, like: "don't tell her you like her too early," "don't give her compliments," "don't be the one to initiate a conversation," and the list goes on for miles. It's all bullshit. When you start playing games, you stop being real.

The way I view emotional expression is like this: imagine that feeling you have, when you like someone and you don't express it.

It's horrible. The weight of the world is on your shoulders, you're walking around with this huge thing on your back, and you haven't expressed it to anyone. It's just sitting there, all bundled up and you're asking, "What the hell do I do?" TELL HER.

Don't be afraid of being rejected. Fuck that. You've been dealing with all these feelings you have for someone... fuck it. Hand them over. Now SHE gets to deal with them. If she rejects you, that's fine. She can set that bag of feelings down on the ground, walk away, and neither one of you are hurt... but she is going to be the one to deal with it now.

Maybe that's selfish, but I look at it much differently than most people. I'm not weak if I express myself. I'm not weak if I tell a woman how I feel. No way.

> "Here, you deal with it. I'm into you. I like you. I want to be around you. I don't know how you feel, but I don't really give a fuck. Deal with that reality."

Now it's on her. Now she can decide what she wants to do with that. Put that responsibility elsewhere.

That's where you take expressing your feelings and emotions from being a "weak" or "beta" thing, to being a man. Men don't have to hide their emotions. Hiding that shit makes you a pussy. A man expresses himself sincerely, puts it out there, and whether he gets rejected or accepted doesn't really matter. The point is that he has the balls to put himself out there.

Rejection is a bigger indictment of the person who rejects you than it is you. It doesn't make her a bad person; it just means it's about her. It's not about you – especially when, as I said, you come from a strong, sincere standpoint and not a desperate, weak, pansy, "nice guy" standpoint.

Please do these exercises. Write the letters. Burn them. Do the mirror exercise, every single day. You'll feel a million times better for having done it. If it feels silly or ridiculous to you at first, that's all the more reason to keep doing it.

Wherever you are in your life, even if you think you've already achieved it all, there is no shame in doing this stuff. I still do it myself periodically, just to make sure I'm always running from a neutral place, and I'm not carrying any baggage or old shit with me.

THE ROLE OF
MALE SEXUAL ENERGY

Romance isn't about an end result. It's about a series of moments that remind us what all of the pain was for. I've been fortunate to have loved plenty, and even though it didn't work out, I was always able to create moments that lasted a lifetime. Sometimes it's more important to have been memorable than anything else. At the end of your life will be an entire scrapbook of memories, but the ones that mean the most transcend time and allow us to feel truly loved.

I would like to take this opportunity to explain one of the most critical aspects of my personality – the aspect that is the driving force behind the majority of my successes in life – sexual energy. I utilize my sexual energy and love more than any other qualities aside from my humor. My mindset in life is derived from a very sincere desire to bring about pleasure in others' lives.

This doesn't necessarily mean in a sexual way; however, the two do have a very close relationship. I want to introduce some ideas to the male members of my audience about utilizing their sexual energy and creating a passionate, loving relationship with that special someone (or someones) in their lives.

Let me start by saying that any tricks, moves, positions, toys or whatever else you use in the bedroom will pale in comparison to what you can accomplish if you firstly stimulate her mentally by harnessing your sexual energy.

Anticipation, sincerity, passion, strength, good hygiene, assertiveness, humility, humor and inner love are all the things that make women melt. They're characteristics that, if willingly expressed in a fearless way, will prepare your woman for whatever you decide to do to her physically.

I am, by my own admission, a pleasure delayer. Rarely do I hook up with or fuck women that I just met. It's not really my style. I prefer the mental aspect. I want to climb inside her head, heart and soul long before conquering her pussy.

The mental aspect of being sexual is the catalyst for all other facets of the relationship. If you're not familiar with the term "pleasure delayer," it's a man/woman who prefers to allow sexual tension to grow and grow through flirting, deep conversations, connecting and light touching… until one day, the dam behind her panties cannot be contained any longer, and you have no choice but to act on the physical.

I tell the women I'm interested in that I'm going to do this. I am not ashamed of these desires, sexual prowess or the methods I implement to achieve them. Most women are generally taken aback by this approach. I am direct to the point of awkwardness… and I love awkwardness. I am the master of taking the most intensely uncomfortable situation and making light of it.

The sexual energy I express toward a woman is a sincere interest in her "being" as well as the strong desire to play in her "energy." I know what you're thinking: "What the fuck does he mean, play in her energy!?"

Let me explain…

We've all got our "bubble" that keeps us safe. It's the bubble of energy that, when entered by another human being, results in the heart rate accelerating, breath shortening and sweat glands perspiring. It's a very deliberate physical response to someone being in our "space."

My goal, when meeting a woman or talking to a woman whom I desire to seduce, is to ever so slowly and deliberately familiarize myself within her energy. Most men have no tact and thusly screw up any chances of having a good sexual encounter simply because they move too quickly.

I'm not talking about some kind of bullshit "PUA" pick up artist type advice. What I'm suggesting should be used and applied even in long-term relationships.

I've never had a relationship fizzle sexually. The main reason is that I never let the woman I'm with feel like her life is redundant or passionless. Every time I fuck her, I try to make it different. I try to please her in ways that she's only read in trashy romance novels, and I make sure she's aware of my sexual energy at all times.

Whether you're in a long-term relationship or just getting to know a woman, make it your goal to slowly ease yourself into her "energy" or "space" and then stay there.

I usually will do this gradually while we're talking. I'll move ever so slightly until the heat from our bodies has met. I'll remain in that spot for a few minutes but won't actually touch her. She doesn't get to touch me yet... and that's part of the anticipation. This is what gets women going: anticipation, patience, control, dominance.

After a few minutes of being in her bubble, I'll begin to mimic her breathing. Typically, the only time your breathing is in sync with another is when you're fucking. Women know this subconsciously. I breathe with them while I'm listening to what they're talking about and looking them in the eye.

Then...

I back off. I pull my energy back out of her bubble, so the heat is no longer there. I deliberately cool things off in an abrupt fashion. I want her to be aware of my energy, and sometimes that means pulling it away so quickly that she can actually feel it leave.

I'll do that several times while having a conversation, allowing our energies to begin mingling and meshing while we converse, then abruptly pulling away.

After the third or fourth time, she'll have subconsciously picked up on it and that's when she begins to move into my energy field. She does not want to be out of my energy.

My sexual energy is warm, strong and authentic. She knows it and after a short time, she comes to crave it.

We will do this dance for as long as I feel is necessary until I can actually see her losing her breath and her head beginning to perspire.

This is Seduction 101.

If you're in a long-term relationship, it's **CRITICAL** that you do the above. You cannot let the passion die. Sexual passion is paramount to a strong, healthy relationship.

Explore your woman's energy, take your time.

The key is to condition yourself to be strong, patient and dominant with your woman outside of the bedroom. She'll literally be ready to let you inside her sugar walls damn near anytime you please if your energy remains intertwined with hers.

All of the nasty shit you've been fantasizing about having her do, she'll be doing, and you won't even have to suggest it. Her number one goal will become to please you, because she adores the time you take to fuck her both mentally and physically.

Most women want to feel dominated. They want to feel "small" and "safe." In my experience, the stronger and more empowered the woman, the more she craves a force bigger than herself to share her life with. Women do not want weak, timid or spineless men.

The only women who do want that type of partner are women with self-esteem issues who require someone to control. The same goes for men. They want a woman who is strong, maternal and loving yet capable of being naughty. If a man desires a "doormat" for a partner, it's because of his own insecurities.

I've written before about "maintaining" your edge in a relationship, as a man. There are several ways to do so, such as being a loving father, capable provider and respected member of the community. However, the absolute most effective manner I've found is to be all of the above and then, when it's just the two of you, you're her "sexual warrior."

You dominate her in such a way that is not demeaning, but rather confirmation of the wonderful choice she made in choosing you as her mate. As I've written above, it starts with her mind.

Throughout the day, you should be whispering nasty suggestions in her ear. I have no shame in doing so… I'll set her breakfast in front of her, lean down to kiss her on the cheek and whisper in her ear that, "I can still taste you on my lips from last night." Then I go about my morning as if I said nothing.

Daily little gestures such as the above will have a profound effect on your relationship. This does come with one caveat; if you can't "deliver" on the expectations you've built up throughout the day and in earlier conversations, this WILL NOT WORK.

If you think you're not handling business adequately, I would encourage you to study and communicate with your partner about what she likes so that you are meeting the expectations you've created. The following chapter is also going to be of vital importance in this regard.

TOP TEN WAYS
TO SEX HER RIGHT

Before we start our journey into the mind and vagina of the female species, I'm going to put out a disclaimer. As a writer who enjoys producing a diverse amount of material for damn near any situation, I do draw a quite diverse crowd, and some individuals in this crowd like to pretend they don't like to fuck. They are offended by my language, content and overall demeanor. I also have a following that reads my stuff strictly for empowerment, and I love you for that. However, I DO NOT want to hurt anyone's "wittle feelers" with this chapter.

If you don't like the words "fuck," "pussy," "cock," "balls," "ass," "vagina," or "blowjob," I would **STRONGLY** suggest you discontinue reading right now. (Also, if you're related to me, this could get uncomfortable, so feel free to skip this chapter).

I promise the remainder of the book will have plenty of "PG" material… but right now we're going to get down and dirty on a subject with which many people could use some assistance. As usual, I promise to be informative, funny and above all, functional.

The last chapter primarily addressed attraction, anticipation, energy and seduction. This chapter will more or less cover the "How-to's" of fucking your woman so good that it takes your relationship to a whole other level. Now that we've got the entire preface out of the way, let's get rocking and rolling…

Tip #1 – Trust

I'm making "trust" the very first tip because it is the basis of everything sexually. Having trust in sex is not the same as having trust in other facets of life or relationships (though it does help if you've got it.)

I can meet a woman at a bar, have a great conversation and take her home that evening. She more than likely doesn't "trust" me in the traditional sense of the word. Who can blame her? She doesn't really know me, and we have no history.

However, once we've begun fooling around, I can establish her "sexual trust" while in the midst of foreplay. She does not have to trust me to feed her dog, to not embarrass her in front of her in-laws or to not burn down her house. The only thing she has to trust me to do is to make her cum. Hard, long... and ideally, repeatedly.

The way we establish that sexual trust is by immediately making the experience about **HER**. You're there to fuck **HER**. You're there to please **HER**. You're there to be **HER** fantasy. You express those intentions through your physical actions. I personally am a very dominant and assertive male. I initiate the first kiss. I pick where and how the experience begins. I decide, "Am I going to fuck her on the couch or do I want to pick her up and take her to the bedroom?" I escalate the experience.

NOT HER. (I'm not saying a woman can't switch things up and be the aggressor, but this chapter isn't about seducing a man. It's about fucking your woman senseless.)

She is no longer in control. During sex, the sense of losing control is what makes women wetter than any toy you could hope to buy. Women want to be led sexually.

Side note: In my experience, I have found that the more dominant and assertive a woman is outside of the bedroom, the more passive, submissive and obedient she is inside the bedroom. I don't mean that in a derogatory way. However, that lawyer, manager, model, athlete you've been crushing on who dominates the conversation and hires/fires people all day generally does not want to take you home and then have to tell you how to fuck her. She wants to be absolutely dominated. Often, the bedroom is the only place that she has an opportunity to allow someone else to be in charge.

DO NOT DISAPPOINT! Even if you don't have the biggest cock, you better toss her around and beat that shit up like you were Lexington Steele. Be warned, if you don't, with that particular woman, she'll never call you again. Ever. She'll call me. (Just kidding… except not really.)

Tip #2 – Technique

Now one thing I'd like to mention here is that technique is going to be different depending on a few things that none of us have control over, namely: the size of your dick and the depth of her vagina. There are certain positions and angles that not everyone can accomplish. Sometimes it's because you aren't big enough. Sometimes it's because you're too big or she's too tight.

For that reason, I'm going to try to focus more on hand technique, placement and where to apply pressure. These are maneuvers that can work regardless of whether you're packing heat or are on the smaller side.

I use a lot of hand play in and around the neck, hips and tits. At no point do I want her to feel like I'm just pumping away like some kind of drunken frat boy. You've got to stimulate all of her senses at the same time – the reason being that you're trying to allow her to lose herself in the moment. Once she's lost herself in the moment, she'll relax. Once she is relaxed, the likelihood of her having an orgasm and a memorable experience increases exponentially.

The next time you're climbing on top of your woman and into the missionary position, don't just stick it in. Tease her with the head of your cock. If you're fortunate enough to have a "heavy" or well-endowed dick, smack it against her pussy a little bit. Make her beg for it. Make her reach down and try to shove it in. (And she will try to shove it in!) Don't let her. Take it back away... tease her with it while you rub her clit with your thumb and stroke yourself in front of her.

Then, once you've decided she's had enough and has earned what's coming next... stick it in. You've got to continue to stimulate her senses. Slowly lower yourself down on her, and allow her to feel your breath against her neck. Don't thrust it all the way in yet. Take your left hand and put it on her hip. GRAB it. Don't gently grip it with a dainty touch. This moment is when you establish who is in charge.

GRAB HER FUCKING HIP.

Then slowly, using her hip as leverage, pull her pussy onto you. Keep being patient. She's going to try to tear into you, but she's not the one in charge. You are. You dictate how and when she cums.

With your right hand, grip the back of her neck. Make sure your hand placement is slightly lower, almost on the trap muscles. I like to begin massaging the woman's neck as I ease myself in. Typically it's out of necessity as she adjusts to my size. (I will talk more about this later when I get to doggy style.) This also goes back to the point I was making about helping her relax. I massage her neck because I'm about to massage her insides. In order for the entire body to be in unity, you've got to put it there. If at any point she feels "detached" from the experience or her pussy… its game over.

Tip #3 – Visuals

Contrary to popular belief, women are very visual and even more so during sex. It is your responsibility to give her something to look at. If you're fat as fuck, she's not going to enjoy watching you pound her. However, this chapter is not about fat loss. (We'll touch on health and fitness in subsequent chapters.)

I will, however, offer some guidance for our heavier set men who've already got the beer gut going on. You aren't going to lose that gut over night. Realistically, it's going to take months. In the meantime, your focus at the gym is building big shoulders, chest, traps, arms and back. Obviously, I would encourage you to work your entire body, but the reason I mention those muscles is that if you've got a gut, she's going to want to put her eyes somewhere else.

If you take the time to build a big neck/shoulders/chest and arms, it gives her bulging shoulders to look at and strong arms to hold onto. It's not a permanent solution, but it buys you some time while you get rid of that nasty gut. The same approach can be applied if you're super skinny; focus on the same muscle groups, and it'll work like a charm.

Another trick I like to use while focusing on the visual is to make her watch. I usually do this in the very beginning, especially as I enter her for the first time, and then I'll do it again later when I'm pounding her. Take your dominant hand and reach gently behind her head. Simultaneously, as you elevate her head with that hand, take your other hand and press gently down on one of her hips. I force her gaze upon my cock as it's sliding inside of her.

Some women (who am I kidding) **MOST** women are very insecure, sexually. They feel "ashamed" if they get caught looking during sex. All I do is eliminate the problem. I know she wants to watch. I know she's a freak who wants to watch herself getting fucked. I simply accommodate that desire and take the insecurity out of the equation by being the one that forces her gaze. (What can I say? I'm thoughtful!) This also goes back to being the "leader" and gaining her trust.

Tip #4 – Doggy Style

Many of the women you have sex with will **ONLY** cum while in this position, and many more will ask to cum from this position because it's easier to access the "G-Spot" versus the clit and provides a different type of orgasm.

Either way, I've got a few tricks that you can use from here that will drive her absolutely insane.

Firstly, when you put her into this position, we're going do something she's probably never had done to her (here comes the personal trainer anatomy lesson.) You are going to firmly grip her lower back just at the top of her ass. Try to grab a little further to the outside than you would normally grip. You're doing this because you want your thumbs to rest right where the sciatic nerve is located.

The sciatic nerves run down each leg, and their beginning points lie beneath the piriformis muscle. (This is the muscle connecting the ass to the lower back on either side of her spine.) You want to put your thumb in that spot on either side of her ass/hips. Begin massaging in a circular motion and pressing fairly hard as you slide inside of her.

What's going to happen is that the sciatic nerve will begin to release tension all down her legs, lower back and subsequently, her pussy.

If you've got a small dick, this is going to allow her to relax the muscles within her vagina so that you can go deeper than you might have otherwise been able.

If you have a big dick, doing this will open her up so that you can go balls deep without her feeling like she can't handle you. It's also psychological; the second you show any knowledge of the female body and her pressure points during sex, she's going to let out the deepest, loudest moan you've ever heard.

Most women expect you to be stupid and caveman like. When you massage that spot as you begin slowly working her from behind, her body will literally melt. It's usually not more than a few strokes before she's reaching down and rubbing her clit or playing with her own nipples.

It's money. I guarantee it.

Tip #5 – Switch It Up

Fucking, making love, sex, intercourse or whatever you want to call it is much like dancing. You've got to have more than a few moves and good rhythm. She shouldn't know exactly what's coming next. Predictability will kill the mood. Switch it up. Switch up your pace. Switch up positions. Switch up angles. Switch up how you kiss her. Switch up your stroke. Switch up your grip. Switch up your language (yeah, learn to talk dirty.)

I will give you one warning with "switching it up."

DO NOT SWITCH IT UP IF SHE'S ABOUT TO CUM!

She will literally punch you in the dick and think you're some kind of spastic, sexually immature tool bag if you do this. When you're tearing that ass up and her breathing is getting deeper, she's getting louder, and you feel her pussy clenching, it means you're doing it correctly. Don't fuck it up now by ruining her orgasm.

If none of that is happening, feel free to switch it up. You don't want her to go silent! (Unless she's cumming – some women do that.) You've got to train yourself to pay attention to her physical, verbal and energetic cues, especially if she's not loud to begin with.

She'll let you know if her pussy is getting numb from you pounding it. If she was once moaning and is now just sort of taking it, she more than likely is losing feeling. Immediately withdraw and begin gently eating her pussy. Maybe wipe away the wetness so that she can begin getting feeling back. You didn't fuck up the experience, but you came dangerously close.

As I mentioned earlier, you're trying to get your woman to lose complete control. That means forgetting the time, forgetting the place, forgetting her inhibitions, forgetting that you forgot to do the fucking dishes for the third time this week! (Just kidding... why would **YOU** be doing the dishes???? Again, kidding! Calm down ladies!)

Tip # 6 – Smell Amazing

We're sticking with the theme of the different "senses." If you smell like a bum's nut-sack, her pussy will dry up like the Sahara Desert faster than you can even imagine. Your stank ass will be the only thing she remembers from having sex with you… that pungent, sweaty mess, just pumping away on top of her. It won't matter how big you were or how well you ate her pussy. The first thing she'll tell her friends is…

> "Guuuurl! This fool had a beautiful dick, ate it right, but that fool smelled so bad I thought I was fucking a pile of dirty gym socks!"

I am not an expert in colognes. The last few years, I was on that poverty time and didn't have the luxury of trying out multiple brands. I will say, however, that I always thoroughly wash, wear deodorant that goes well with my body's natural fragrance, and I own one or two decent colognes.

If you need help picking out fragrances, I would suggest going down to a department store and trying some. (Besides, they've got hot chicks that work in those places, and you can ask her what scent she prefers on a man who's on top of her.)

Tip #7 – Hair Pulling

We're starting to get into more advanced maneuvers during sex. If these are not things you usually do during sex, I would advise you to proceed with caution. If you fuck some of these tricks up, you'll kill the vibe.

Hair pulling is a technique. Firstly, grab an entire handful of it! If you pull on a few individual strands, it hurts like a bitch, and you're just going to piss her off. She's also going to know that this is **NOT** something you've done before, and nobody wants to have sex with an amateur! (Except for men… they love training amateurs.)

Next, when you're pulling her hair, you've got to know how much pressure to apply. This is going to be largely contingent on the type of woman you're dealing with. Some like their hair gently pulled because they've got sensitive scalps. Much like grabbing too little hair, yanking too hard could hurt like hell and kill the mood.

Other women LOVE having their hair pulled to the point that you're looking down into her eyes while going balls deep. The bottom line is that you're going to have to gauge what turns her on. Don't be afraid to ask while fucking her.

This leads us to our next highly delicate "tip."

Tip #8 – Spanking

This is one of those moves that's either going to be a home-run or it'll bring the entire session to an abrupt end. You had better know what kind of woman you're dealing with prior to smacking the fuck out of her ass.

I prefer a more direct approach; if I can't already tell, I ask. Usually, I'll try to work the question in during foreplay or dinner (if the topic of sex is brought up.)

Spanking during sex is another move where any apprehension will be immediately evident during your futile attempt. If you're going to spank her, fucking SPANK HER! It doesn't even matter if it's hard or soft, but you'd better have some confidence prior to doing so.

Spanking is right up there with slapping, whether it's in the face, her ass, tits, pussy, whatever. Some women are into different things and like to feel like they're being completely dominated and tossed around. Not only that, but the longer you're with someone, the more likely that they're going to allow you to experiment and try new things.

Have fun with it, but remember that the more aggressive you get, the more necessary communication becomes. Be verbal, be sincere and be attentive.

That brings us to our next taboo sex tip. Perhaps you're noticing that we're getting progressively dirtier. If you're still reading, it probably means you're a true fan. I figure if I've offended anyone, they've stopped reading about nine chapters ago.

Tip #9 – Choking

I am warning you right now: if you use this on a chick who has been sexually abused, doesn't trust you or is potentially "new" with you… you are asking for trouble. Unless, of course, she's told you previously that she likes it.

Choking a woman during sex or more specifically, when she's cumming, is a delicate and advanced maneuver. If you bust this out on a woman whom isn't into it, you run a serious risk of getting punched in the face, ending a relationship or a whole host of other issues.

As I've said before, **COMMUNICATION IS KEY!!!!!** When in doubt, ASK! The women who do enjoy being choked do not want you pressing on their windpipe directly with your thumb or fingers.

You want to evenly distribute the pressure across her throat, squeezing inward and increasing pressure as she approaches orgasm. This technique allows you to cuts off the air/blood to her head, and you can dictate how much/little to allow – this should be decided based on her reactions.

I had one woman who liked to be choked to the point of almost passing out while she came. This took significant time and focus to work up to. We had a healthy sexual relationship and progressed to the point that I knew exactly when to let go to allow her to catch her breath, and when to tighten because it was providing her maximum pleasure.

Practice, communicate and err on the side of caution. She'll understand if you hold back with this move, as it is an extremely individualized thing.

Tip #10 – Eating Pussy

"Brenden, why did you wait until the very end to explain something that should have been put at the very beginning!?"

I'll tell you why… because out of all of the sex tips I've just given you, this is far and away going to be the most descriptive. This is the only safe place to put this!

Eating good pussy means losing all inhibitions. If you try to nibble on it as if it's the food on your plate you've been avoiding, you'll kill the fucking vibe. Same for you, ladies! If you're treating a dick like it's made out of nine-day-old macaroni salad, we're going to know… and then we're going to tell our friends that you give terrible head.

First things first... everyone is different. I like to start by running my tongue up the thighs, beginning at her knee. If I'm taking her shoes/boots off, I'll start around the ankle.

I also like to begin this process BEFORE the panties have come off. Start by kissing the inside of her thighs while you allow your thumb to gently caress her pussy. Place the thumb firmly where her clit is located over her panties and begin rubbing in a circular fashion. While doing this, begin breathing directly onto her pussy as you massage her thighs with your other hand.

You're building anticipation and within seconds, her panties should be soaked. Remove the panties and put both hands behind her knees. Gently and firmly force her legs up around her ears, exposing her entire vagina and ass.

(This next tip is NOT for the squeamish. Not every dude is into this and if you're not, no big deal... just know that you're a pussy.)

Lick her ass all the way up to her clit in one single motion. Make sure this chick has showered or at least cleaned recently. I'm serious; you've got to use your own discretion here. If you're a freak like me, you'll just dive in... but not everyone is like that.

Next, once you've reached the clit, gently start sucking on it. Hand placement is the key. I like to hold one leg up behind the knee, and then grab a breast with the opposite hand so I can play with her nipples. Sex and eating pussy are basically "Multi-tasking 101."

That's as far as I'm taking you with oral sex. I could go further, but that should be more than enough to get you started. Frankly, everything after this is just a bonus. Just remember, stay near the clit, gauge her sensitivity when licking/sucking on it and enjoy yourself.

Wow! If you've read this far, you've basically gone through a four thousand word essay on fucking Brenden. I sincerely hope this helps many of you men out there with wives and girlfriends.

If I were to leave you with one last "tip," it'd be this:

Having amazing sex and being a god in the bedroom begins and ends with a sincere desire to make someone feel good. It's the most raw and honest expression of love. Taking your time, being deliberate and thoughtful are all ways of expressing love even if you aren't "in love."

YOUR JOB IS TO NOT FUCK UP YOUR KIDS

As a man who was raised by a single mother, I take great pride in being able to be a strong, loving force for my children. My kids are the best thing that's ever happened to me... they're my best friends and my reason for working hard. If you haven't already, I hope all of you are blessed enough to have children someday.

There, I said it. Don't fuck up your kids. Many of you reading this are thinking, "Why, whatever do you mean, Brenden?" I mean that your kids were perfect when they came into this world. Any issues they develop afterward (aside from genetic/mental/physical) are squarely your fault.

It hurts hearing that I'm sure, but it's true. If your kids suck, it's because you suck. The good news is that's it's not too late – unless they're teenagers, then you're probably fucked. Thankfully, your children are incredibly impressionable up until about twelve years old. Then they stop giving a shit what you say, so if your little bastard is approaching that age, you better get your ass in gear.

"Who the fuck does this guy think he is?"

I'll tell you who I am... I'm the parent who has three amazingly well-behaved children. I'm the parent whose one-year-old is watching your seven-year-old act like an asshole at the store while you futilely count to five. I'm the parent who manages all three children at the grocery store with little to no effort. I'm the parent who's been taking his daughters to fine dining establishments since they were little for "date-night" and never had a single incident.

If your children are well behaved, articulate, have manners and other people approach you regularly to compliment you, I'm not talking to you (although, you may want to keep reading because this shit is going to get funny!)

If, however, you're the parent I described — the parent who cringes at the thought of dragging your "Bebe" ass kids into the grocery store — then listen up! You're going to have to start being a stronger leader. Your children's future depends on it.

As a personal trainer of thirteen years, a Rottweiler owner of eleven years and a parent of ten years, I'm speaking with plenty of experience in the field of getting people/animals to do what I want. I lump dogs and kids together, along with grown ass personal training clients, because ultimately they all require the **EXACT** same thing when being trained: will.

Let me repeat that: WILL. The key to altering your child's behavior is establishing that you've got an unbreakable will.

Your children must know that when the line has been drawn, it is immovable. "My mommy/daddy doesn't ever back off from that line no matter what I do."

Once you've established the will, you must establish the consistency. I begin teaching my children very early... like we're talking "infant" early. My son is one, and he already knows daddy's boundaries. Not because I'm mean or violent, but because he knows I will punish him without emotion or afterthought.

"Brenden, how/why do you punish a one year old?"

Behavior is a learned experience. I know my son, and I know when he's got a legit gripe and when he's just trying to be a little pain in the ass. The moment I recognize his acting out or testing me, I simply pick him up, put him on time-out and walk away.

I don't say shit. I don't explain why he's there or what he did wrong. He's one. He doesn't have the capacity to rationalize what just happened. All he needs to know is, "Wow, when I try to put metal objects up the dog's nose, my Dad tells me 'no' and puts me in my crib."

That's it. He doesn't need to understand anything at the age of one, other than the most basic of things: "When mom/dad says no, that's it." The reason I start this method of parenting so early is because raising children is like building a house. I'm laying a strong foundation so that they understand what type of behavior is expected of them and what won't be tolerated… ever.

So first, we established our will. We then combined it with consistency. Now we're going to add in the final element, which is love.

"But Brenden, I do love my kids!"

Do you? Do you listen to them when they're talking? Do you allow them to explain in broken English what happened on the swing set? Are you busy texting, working, cooking, watching television and just nodding your head?

Your kids know when you don't give a shit about what they're saying. If you won't listen to the gossip that's happening on the playground, they're certainly not going to be telling you about how they're pregnant at sixteen years old and don't know what to do... and don't bother being angry when they don't, because it's your fault. Never forget that.

Children will tell you everything from the time they speak until they're grown adults with their own families if they feel like you actually give a shit and listen. If you're an inconsiderate listener and have issues staying present, don't be surprised when they stop talking to you.

My children all know that "Daddy doesn't mess around." However, they also know that Daddy learned from the best (my mom,) and so he gives freely, rewards without warning and always (always!) has their best interests in mind. When your children trust you and love you, they'll respect you.

Having your children's respect is **CRITICAL** to their development as well-rounded people. If mommy is willing to date an abusive prick that is always kicking her ass, guess what your daughter is learning is acceptable behavior in a relationship?

If you're a man who is dating/married to a woman who is constantly nagging, belittling and disrespecting him in front of his son... guess what kind of woman "little Billy" is going to wind up marrying?

Your children are watching you. They're relying on you to show them what is and isn't acceptable. Being an amazing parent and raising thoughtful, productive, happy people is about being one. The second you became a parent, your entire mindset should have shifted. **YOU** must be more. **YOU** must be better. **YOU** must be an example.

I've been through one official divorce and had another separation. I've got three children from two different women. I ended those toxic relationships because they were just that... toxic.

The first relationship with my daughters' mother had been a very loving, friendship-based romance for six years. However, we got together very young and had a family of five by twenty-five years old. Ultimately, our values weren't consistent and the relationship ended.

I knew that there would be a social stigma or blowback from leaving the mother of my two daughters. I knew that the criticism would be loud and that outsiders wouldn't understand. However, one thought anchored me to the decision that I could not shake:

"If my daughters ever find themselves in an unhealthy, toxic relationship, do I want them to have the strength and courage to pursue their happiness no matter what the public perception? Or do I want them to stick it out for fear of judgment and condemnation?"

Once I asked myself that question, it made the decision easy. I want all of my kids to know that being miserable for fear of judgment is something that only weak, insecure people do. Strong, respectable leaders make the difficult choice to pursue their happiness regardless of what others think.

The point I'm trying to illustrate is that you owe it to your children, yourself and society to raise quality offspring. It starts and ends with **YOU**. When you commit to the personal growth, your goals and consistently strive to be more… your kids will see that, respect it and hopefully emulate it.

MY TOUGHEST ANGEL

HONORING YOUR CHILDREN AS
INDIVIDUALS

As parents, we must recognize the strengths and weaknesses of each of our children. It's far too easy to fall into the trap of drawing unfair comparisons that deliver a harsh, albeit unintentional, blow to a child's self-image. Honor your children's individual strengths, talents and passions, and encourage them to improve upon their weaknesses without using a sibling or peer to "set the bar." Allow each child's "best" to be her own, absent comparison to another.

As a father of three, I get asked about the differences between all of my children. Often, I am in awe at just how unique, yet very much the same, each of them is. I think, as parents, it requires a conscious effort to not compare our children to one another, simply because doing so is human nature. When we observe a desirable behavior in one child, it's normal to expect the same of our other children.

Obviously, this thinking can be "good" from an educational standpoint... to a degree. However, it's also a slippery slope. It is critical that when parenting, you not alienate your children by viewing them as one cohesive unit, rather than the special individuals they are.

My daughter Jasmine is a prime example of a child who walks to the beat of her own drum, and as a father, I couldn't be more proud. Jasmine fearlessly expresses herself. She does what I teach daily, naturally. Her energy and "spark" are so completely different than my other children and different than most people in general. She might be one of the funniest people (not just child) that I've ever known. Her sense of humor, combined with her ability to thin-slice most situations, makes her jokes incredibly "smart" for a child her age.

One afternoon, Sophia and Jasmine were riding in the car with their Nana. The girls were in the backseat watching movies when my mom pulled alongside another vehicle at a red light. The "woman" sitting in the driver's seat was noticeably different than other drivers. This fact was not lost upon Jasmine, who quickly spouted, "Look Nana, a she-bro!"

My mom, not knowing what she was talking about, looked to her right and saw the "woman." My mom recognized that this was a transgender woman. However, she didn't understand what Jasmine was saying, so she asked, "What's a she-bro, Jasmine?" Immediately, Jasmine shot back, "A she-bro is a SHE that looks like a BRO!" My mom nearly died of laughter. This is a prime example of the way Jasmine's sense of humor works! She wasn't trying to be cruel or inappropriate – she just looked, saw a "woman" and thought she looked like a "bro."

By contrast, Sophia would never dream of saying something like that. She might think to herself, "Wow, something is different with that lady?" and then proceed to ask about it. It would never occur to her to combine those thoughts and crack a joke.

As I continue to parent all of my children, their individual strengths and weaknesses are constantly on display, and as their father, I do my best to accentuate their strengths and positive attributes while promoting the growth of their weaker characteristics.

Where Sophia would choose to be diplomatic and sensitive, Jasmine will deliver the cold hard truth in such an authentic way that it forces people to consider her words. (Wonder where she gets that!?) My son, Phoenix, does varying degrees of both, and I remain curious to see his development in that regard.

Not every child is going to be a bookworm, just as they aren't all going to be star athletes. My daughter Sophia creates beautiful artwork and has an energy that will illuminate the world. Jasmine will light up the world with her humor. As parents, we must remember to respect our children's differences – both the differences from their siblings, as well as from us.

I often see bits of myself in Sophia, as she shares my intuition and possesses an incredible sense of empathy. She gives of herself so willingly, often leaving her exposed and vulnerable. I worry that the world won't always understand her light and love.

I see parts of their mother in both of my daughters, some good and some bad. I do my best not to "judge" these characteristics with statements like, "You're just like your mother!" Of course your kids are going to be like their other parent... they've got the same blood coursing through their veins.

I continue to learn from all of my kids, but it's my toughest angel, Jasmine, who holds me accountable to my authenticity and honesty. While Sophia forces me to be more reflective and thoughtful with my words, it is Jasmine who inspires me to continue to deliver the occasionally necessary proverbial "bitch slap" that those around me might need.

BEYOND "SURVIVING"
AS A SINGLE PARENT

Too little too late, can't forget the past, letting go of a future that never came to pass. Beautiful babies and hard lessons learned, our words carried power and bridges were burned. When sorry isn't a big enough word, and I love you loses its meaning, today this closet gets a proper cleaning.

No longer filled with anger, my heart is full of love, drawing on power from the force up above. Wondering if they see me the way I see myself, or has the perception been changed now that I've been placed upon the shelf.

The previous chapters covered some of the "how-to's" of parenting. I'm not going to revisit that here. Rather, I want to discuss the psychology of being single parents and how to overcome a lot of the fear associated with such endeavors.

You're going to be unfairly judged (get over it!) and many are going to gaze upon you with pity. (Don't mind those assholes either!) The weight of the world is NOT, in fact, on your shoulders.

Your job, while slightly more complicated, is still the same as it ever was. **HONOR YOURSELF** and the rest will take care of itself. Most single parents get in the habit of saying shit like…

"My son/daughter always comes first, no matter what!"

WRONG! I understand the sentiment, and I certainly get how politically correct it is to make such statements, but it's completely untrue and totally ass backwards. Your responsibility is to set an example for your children. Teach them to honor themselves by first honoring yourself.

Single parents everywhere have been conditioned with this idea that they themselves can't be happy or "selfish," for fear of being perceived as a bad parent. I have news for you… kids grow up. When they get to be teenagers, they're going to have their own lives and goals.

If you don't honor yourself now, you'll be left alone, depressed, with nothing going on in your life and an overwhelming sense of abandonment as your child grows and begins living his or her own life. Don't be that guy/woman.

Single parents must realize that your goals, dreams and aspirations are even more important once you're a parent. They're not to be diminished. I'm not saying you should be reckless or anything like that. However, don't be afraid to continue aspiring for more.

Don't be fearful that you can't achieve your career goals, love goals and fitness goals. You can and do have the opportunity to do all of that and then some... the only difference is your "fan base" just grew by one. Not to mention, you now have someone holding you accountable to those goals/dreams.

Thankfully, I learned from the best in regards to "honoring myself." I was raised (for the most part) by a single mother. My mom grew up in Alaska, with no running water and at times with no electricity. She got pregnant and had me just two months shy of her nineteenth birthday.

My mom had no higher education, never made much of an income at any of her jobs, and yet, she went on to become a self-made multi-millionaire as a business owner, motivational speaker, author and entrepreneur. She was/is the epitome of what it means to be a single parent and still excel in life. She is an inspiration to single parents everywhere.

So when I tell you to "honor yourself," I'm not talking out of my ass. I've seen what happens first hand when you do so. I, myself, am currently on a similar path. The motivational seminar/self-help world seems to be something that our family has in its blood. (I'm fully anticipating one of or all of my children participating to some degree.)

Single parents, believe me when I tell you that your goals and dreams aren't "pie in the sky." One of the most challenging endeavors that any of us could take on is raising another human being. While it's true that I am only able to be a "part-time" Dad (thanks, judicial system!) my level of commitment rivals that of most full-time parents.

For example, for the last two years, I've traveled back to California to be with my daughters once a month, every month. I make arrangements for where we're staying, rent a car, buy a plane ticket and plan an entire weekend for us. In addition, I fly them out to see me on spring break, summers and all major holidays. (Thank you to everyone who helps me out with these arrangements… I love you all!)

I do all of this while still coordinating the weekends and weekdays I have my son, as well as working full time, making time for the gym, launching my writing career, dating, etc. The point I'm trying to illustrate is that it's entirely possible to do ALL of it. Single parents can and do have the ability to rise above the adversity and still achieve their goals without sacrificing parenting time.

My mom is the shining example of how honoring yourself can pay off, not just for you as an individual, but by making you a better parent as well. Despite many hardships, she continued to strive for greatness, and in the summer of 1997, went from making no more than thirty thousand dollars a year, to suddenly earning between fifty and two hundred thousand dollars... per month!

My mom had done what nobody in our little town of fifteen thousand people thought possible. She was on her way to being a self-made millionaire! Over the course of the next eighteen months, my mom would make somewhere in the neighborhood of two million dollars.

Our life had shifted permanently: not because of the vast amount of revenue she was earning, but rather because she had permanently changed my thinking about what is possible. It literally blew my mind. My mom had done it. She was a success, with no college education, as a single mother, living in a tiny ass little town.

The parent I am today is a tribute to my mom. I've been able to take all of the lessons she taught me about love, empathy, understanding, discipline, determination and sincere authenticity, and apply them to my relationship with my children. The lessons she taught me are the reason that, despite time constraints and distance, the relationship I have with my kids continues to grow and flourish.

My children have the same trust and faith in me that I have in my mom. That was made possible by the Universe providing me the absolute best teacher imaginable for parenting and life.

Today, I proudly accept who I am and display it thanks to my mom. Even as I move toward the next chapter in my life and venture fearlessly into my thirties, my mom is still my number one friend. She has set a standard for the type of woman I hope to meet some day. Every psychotic, neurotic, selfish, manipulative, immature, gold-digging woman is turned away, as I am constantly reminded by my very own mother that there are amazing women walking this planet.

The idea of settling for anything less seems ridiculous. She has set the bar for me as an author, speaker, parent and entrepreneur as well. With God's grace, I hope to one day reach that bar.

Set the same example for your own children. Show them, in the way you live your own life, that their dreams and passions are worth pursuing – just as yours are. The greatest gift you can give your children is being the best, happiest, healthiest version of YOU possible.

THE "GREAT WHITE" OF BUSINESS

I'm definitely a firm believer of constantly evaluating our own actions and doing our best to determine if they were appropriate. The truth is that some people (like me) are not wired to slow down and explain things. I do my best to blog, share or write as I'm moving one hundred miles per hour through life. However, in business, I am not afforded that luxury. Time is money, and mistakes, politics and other such bullshit only deviate from money-making activities.

There are going to be days that you're going to have to call on your inner "Great White" to deal with life. Sharks can't suddenly stop or swim backwards. They're almost always moving forward, toward the next goal. I'm not saying you shouldn't take time for "reflection," but make sure it's brief and doesn't leave you dwelling on the past or what might have been.

The Great White also draws on its intuition – its ability to sense electromagnetic pulses from any living object. It's "sixth sense" is so accurate that it can sense up to 1/2 a billionth of a volt. This shark does not slow down to ponder, "Hmm… should I not trust my intuition and try another route?"

It has total faith in its ability to locate what it desires even in the darkest of waters. Human beings, through social programming, are extremely indecisive and fearful that they might not make the "right" decision. There are no "right" or "wrong" decisions. The Universe is indifferent.

Good, bad, right and wrong are manmade descriptions of events. The Universe only concerns itself with the "is." The wonderful thing about the "is" is that it's only located in the present moment. In the world of business, this is vitally important.

The majority of the employees I deal with are always looking ahead to better days rather than staying in the present, crushing small goals daily and remaining focused on the task at hand.

The Universe only requires "intent" and "consistency" to manifest what you desire in business. There is no point in dwelling on what "might" happen.

There are going to be casualties while you pursue your dreams in business. Some of those casualties will be friends, co-workers, employees. You will experience the deaths of several relationships.

The loftier your goals, the more casualties you're going to encounter. It's **CRITICAL** that you don't take all of them personally. As long as you're staying true to your values and principles, you cannot dwell on them.

All of us have a choice about our level of involvement in the pursuit of "big dreams." The victories and losses cannot be personalized. Sometimes you're going to be the hammer, and in the beginning, you're going to be the nail. That's how you get good at your business: trial and error.

You will be faced with challenges, setbacks and decisions. Remember the Great White, trust your gut, move forward and do so fearlessly and with purpose.

Realistic expectations

One of the most overlooked aspects of business is setting up realistic expectations. Firstly, let me start by saying that in business, it's critical to do this. The number one reason is so that your ass doesn't get sued.

The last thing you want to do in business, whether it's your own business or in corporate America, is over-promise and then under-deliver. That's how you lose your job and if you were dumb enough to put it in writing, is how you get sued.

Honesty is appreciated by consumers and managers alike. They don't want you to sell them the moon and then deliver Cleveland (no offense to Cleveland intended.) If you can't come through with a particular result, you're much better off saying, "Hey, I can't do XYZ, but I can do this. If that works for you, I'll get working on it." Making that statement sets up an expectation by your boss/customer of what the end result will be.

However, when you don't set realistic expectations, and you say something like, "Hmm... yeah, I can totally get this thing done," only to turn around a few weeks later and say, "Yeah, I don't think this deal is going to work," it makes you look incompetent. With your normal consumer, it may not be an issue. They'll call you an asshole and move on. But if you pull this same stunt with a seasoned business professional, you might find yourself out of business fairly quickly.

Making money isn't rocket science.

It literally begins with a decision. The decision is to stop being so fucking broke. Living paycheck to paycheck sucks. Nobody wants to just "exist" and tiptoe quietly to their grave having achieved little, leaving nothing but debt and a lifetime of struggle behind.

You have to make the decision that this isn't an acceptable narrative for your life. This isn't the way you want to live your life.

Your friends, family, co-workers and pretty much everyone else in your life are going to try to shit on your newfound ambition and ideas. They're going to tell you all of the reasons that it won't work... especially if it's something they don't understand (which is highly likely.)

Well, that's OK. Fuck 'em. You don't need anyone's "approval" to be financially independent. The only one you've got to listen to is you. Hell, even you might be telling yourself that you can't do it. Well pause for a moment and tell that shitty little voice in your head to shut the fuck up. He/she is **NOT** helping your situation.

What will help your situation is having the testicular fortitude to dream and believe that you can achieve lofty financial goals. I don't care if you're sixty-seven with a bad hip and shitty vision or nineteen and still unable to buy beer. The requirements to be financially free and successful are the same.

Make the decision, have an open mind, believe in the ideas, and then go out and do it. If the system is in place, and you're already applying the education and tools, then the only thing that is separating you from your ultimate goal is time. Keep going! Keep grinding! Have faith in your ability to create what you're aspiring for.

DESTROYING CREATIVE BLOCKS

Oh the irony! There I was, going on and on recently about avoiding writer's block and allowing myself to "expand" my content, yada, yada, yada… and lo and behold, I couldn't come up with shit to write today.

"Hello Brenden… Meet Humble Pie!"

Yeah… well save it, "humble pie," because even a case of writer's block isn't going to stop me from knocking out a thousand word shit-tastic chapter today! So without further ado…

Here is how I overcome my writer's block!

Step 1: Get up and move around

You can't accomplish a damn thing just staring at your computer screen. When your "angels," "inspiration" or "creativity" seem to have abandoned you, staring aimlessly at your monitor won't do shit. You've got to re-inspire yourself. Go outside. Walk the block. Don't think about writing. Just observe life, people and the ridiculousness of it all.

I'm fortunate. Thanks to my career, I'm exposed to all sorts of characters who inspire the most insane thoughts on a daily basis. I'd say that ninety percent of my writing comes from conflicts and/or situations that I deal with almost daily.

Step 2: Do NOT edit while you're writing

If you begin editing while attempting to write, you'll just exacerbate the writer's block. Start putting down whatever the hell comes out, and just keep typing. As long as the thoughts are there and your fingers are moving, keep going. It doesn't have to be life altering.

They aren't all going to be "hits." Even the Beatles had some shitty tracks they threw in to make a full album.

The same thing is true for writing. I'm ridiculously critical of my writing and can tell when I'm writing shit and when I'm putting down really solid content. However, one thing that even I must admit... sometimes your most boring, least interesting piece of writing that is spawned from a bad case of writer's block can and will inspire someone out there.

It's the funniest thing too, because I've had people email, text and private message me in response to writing that I considered "sub-par" at best. They'd go on and on about how it really hit home for them and resonated with something they were going through. It really forces you to have a new level of respect for your own creativity, writing and brilliance. Receiving that type of feedback really humbles one to the fact that we don't always understand the significance of our own material – particularly when it manifests while dealing with a creative block.

Totally random, funny story in relation to NOT everything being a hit:

During my senior year of high school, I was dating a lovely young woman whose name will remain anonymous. One Friday night, we decided to go to the movies, and we picked out "Battlefield Earth."

For those who haven't actually seen this movie, let me describe the effect it had on my sweetheart. This film was so bad that about forty-five minutes into it, she asked me if we could leave. Being the stubborn bastard that I am – and probably in part thanks to my OCD about finishing things that I've paid for – I insisted that we stick it out until the end. In my mind, we were already forty-five minutes into this slaptastically stupid-ass sci-fi movie. I'm thinking, "Yeah, we can stick it out... probably another half hour or so left."

WRONG!

That shit-ass film was a hundred and twenty minutes long! We weren't even halfway through this thing. The next seventy-five minutes might have been the longest of my life. About ninety minutes into the movie, she began to cry.

I'm not talking "whining." I mean legitimately crying – tears running down her face, sniffling, can't catch your breath, crying. It was hilarious. John Travolta had made a movie that sucked so much that it made my adorable, sixteen-year-old girlfriend cry as if she was watching her favorite pet get tortured.

Needless to say, the crying only further motivated me to stick it out, because it was the funniest fucking thing I had ever seen. Hell, after a few minutes of her crying and me laughing, she couldn't help but laugh through the tears.

So the next time you think your work sucks, ask yourself...

"Will this be so shitty that by the time someone gets to the end of it, they'll be in actual, physical tears because of how terrible it is?"

If the answer is "no" (which in all likelihood will be the case,) publish that shit and move on with your life.

Step 3: Be Ridiculous

As of this moment riiiiiiight NOW, we're at the seven hundred and eighty five word mark, writer's block be damned! Hopefully you're still reading. Hopefully some of this is going to be useful to you. We've gotten to this point by me being ridiculous and not taking any of this too seriously.

Anxiety, self-criticism and angst will only continue to stifle your creative process. Your writer's block will remain as long as you remain in that state of mind.

You've got to cut yourself some slack and allow the fun and writing to flow out of you.

Besides, what's the worst that could happen? It's not like you'll be making any sixteen-year-old girls cry because of your horrible writing.

PERFECT FAITH

IN AN IMPERFECT WORLD

Create your Universe today through the power of intention coupled with perfect faith. On this day, we give thanks for all that is, was and will be. You're not a victim. You're an empowered, highly intelligent energy with the ability to create your life. You're only limited by your faith and imagination. Perfect faith means eliminating all fear. Fear and faith are polar opposites and neither can exist in the presence of the other.

Sunday remains my favorite day of the week. I can actually feel myself change and evolve through the weekend. By the time Sunday night rolls around, the energy gets to the point that it's almost unbearable. These quiet evenings are when I apply my perfect faith the most.

I am consumed by one overwhelming thought: that something wonderful is about to happen. I live with this singular thought in my head at all times.

Rarely will you ever catch me in a state of "doom" or "anxiety." I have my moments, no doubt… but they are brief, and I always return to neutral quickly.

Maintaining perfect faith while in the midst of chaos and stress is far and away my most valued asset at this particular juncture in my life. I'm not speaking of anything "religious" in the least. I am not versed enough in the many different religions to even venture into that topic. I am, however, quite spiritual.

I was having a conversation recently with a friend of mine about perfect faith and "God." She doesn't have much belief in anything other than what's in front of her, and she expressed to me that she "cringed" every time I used the word "God." I politely explained that I use "God" because it's the most recognizable term among people of faith.

I do not even know if that is the correct name for whatever I believe. If you want the honest truth, I call him "Brenden." I'm being a smart ass... but not really.

The relationship I have with "Energy," "Universe," "God," or "Higher-self" is incredibly difficult to explain. I feel it every second of every single day. Having perfect faith doesn't necessarily mean always making the correct or "moral" decisions. I believe that even in the face of extreme hardship, adversity and stress, the deepest recesses of our being KNOW that all is as it should be – that, to me, is "perfect faith."

I have lived a blessed life. Much of my humility was developed through the realization that many of the problems I've faced were a product of my own decisions. I couldn't help myself. My thirst for knowledge, adventure and experience is second to none.

I know there are many out there like me – people who can't stay in one spot for too long... people who are pushed by an unseen force that drives us to teach, help and inspire. Many more have developed such a feeling of perfect faith as mankind continues toward a "quickening" of sorts. I am proud to express and share this aspect of myself.

My faith is probably my most distinguishable characteristic. From that single trait, all others permeate out. My directness, humor, confidence, humility, sincerity and authenticity all start and end with an undying, unwavering belief in the magic of life.

So many beautiful souls live in absolute fear and terror of their own lives. They fear the world, their decisions and failure. This obsession with fear drives them to be woefully routine and imprisoned in their own minds. They still have "faith," yet it is in an unhealthy way.

These individuals are constantly waiting for the other shoe to drop. They have allowed life to victimize them, to make them weak and scared. There is no benefit to this type of thinking or belief system. It eventually becomes a self-fulfilling prophecy of regret, pain, misery and fear with only glimmers of positive thoughts.

We've all had or have someone in our sphere of influence that acts and behaves in such a way. I find it strange that many people that I associate with daily are of this mind. They do not believe that the Universe or Life is in their corner. Instead, they make decisions based on worst case scenarios and the fear that someone is "getting over on them."

I've dated women who are of this mind. As I grow and spread my wings, they do everything in their power to clip them. They are scared that should I become who I'm supposed to be, I'll realize who they are and leave. The mother of my daughters expressed this exact thought to me in one of her rare moments of honesty. She did not realize that love is synonymous with the word "acceptance." I could not become who I am supposed to be and as a result, "leave her." To do so would mean that I had not reached the place I was seeking.

Instead of simply living life fearlessly, this thought consumed her. She unconsciously sought to break me down. The thought process was, "If I can get him to believe he is something else, he will never grow enough to leave."

Men are notorious for this. I knew a woman who was like a beautiful, wild horse. To watch her run through life was something to behold. She was gorgeous, smart and funny, and she exuded the type of energy that magnetized each and every person to her. She attracted a particular man who was initially intrigued by her energy and beauty.

Unfortunately, after a time together, he realized that her wild spirit illuminated his own shortcomings. He was no longer confident, as her light dwarfed his. They were not of the same mind; therefore, he panicked. Every idea, inspiration and moment of spontaneity she had was rejected, belittled and stifled.

This is what happens when you've outgrown your partner. They will attempt to keep you exactly where you're at. What was once a relationship of support, teamwork and strength is now mired in insecurity. Today is your day of infinite good. Today is the day you give thanks for everything you have in this life. Today we resume our perfect faith in the world and begin running once more.

There is no shame in having faith, and there is no shame in being a "wild horse." We are the movers of the world. Take back that part of you. Do not allow any man, woman or child to tell you differently. Your perfect faith must start and end with you.

Run. Run toward your dreams. Run toward your freedom. Let go of the weight and the negativity. Let go of the doubt, fear and disdain. Forgive yourself for choosing to experience those feelings and run. It's never too late to do so. The people in your life will try to convince you to be sensible and "think things through." Fuck that. Live. Run.

WHEN BEING AWARE IS A PROBLEM

Let me start by saying something that is one hundred percent true and that I'm NOT one hundred percent comfortable with... I piss off a LOT of people. Now I realize that's an incredibly generic statement, and you're sitting there going, "Big fucking deal, Brenden. We all piss off a lot of people!"

I was gifted with an annoyingly strong sense of intuition and empathy that, despite my best attempts, rears its head throughout my business life and makes me aware that I'm angering people.

Let me explain... in business, I'm a hard ass. I've illustrated this in an earlier chapter where I shared a story of evicting a man and telling him he's ruining his life. I negotiate with vendors like they're trying to take my last dime, and I direct employees as if we're on the battlefield. However, despite my deepest desires to "help" and to be "successful," my spiritual side reminds me that I'm being an asshole. Becoming aware of this fact can be quite disheartening.

The rub on being "aware" is that it's synonymous with being "responsible." Once you're responsible, you don't get to be a victim anymore; your excuses no longer carry any weight. I am aware when my behavior is not loving or kind, and there is nowhere to hide from the guilt associated with being responsible.

I can't pretend I'm not the spiritual, love-giving individual that I am. However, I also can't pretend that some people don't suck at business and are going to get steamrolled. That's just the way it is. Those are the rules of the playground we're on, and that aspect of "me" isn't going anywhere.

I have no desire to ascend into some airy-fairy "master" like the Eckhart Tolles of the world. That's not an attack on Tolle; I love his work and it has inspired me greatly. However, I do not ever want to become so high off of my own supply that I start referring to myself as a guru or "expert."

I never want to reach a place where I don't feel comfortable dropping a few "F-bombs" in my writing or conversations for fear that I might fuck up my image or lose money. I want to stand amongst humanity, not above it. So instead of embracing my "spiritual self" or my "cutthroat businessman" entirely, I walk a line that many of us walk: the line of "balance." I earnestly try to remain aware of the spiritual world while doing the dirty work that is necessary to exist on the human plane.

As you expand your "vastness" as a human being and learn more, express more, become aware of more and experience more, you're going to get lost in all of it from time to time. That's where I'm at today… and have been the last couple of days.

Normally, you won't see writers or "experts" opening up this way, but like I said… I know I'm not alone. I know many of you feel conflicted daily over certain aspects of yourself and your personality. I'm letting you know that it's OK. It's normal. It better be, or I'm going to need a fucking straightjacket.

I know many of you who follow my writing might be scratching your head as you're reading this. However, there will be someone, most likely a quiet leader or spiritual person, who will read this and know EXACTLY what I'm talking about – and this is for them.

This Too Shall Pass

In life, you've got a few options. Stay on the shore and try to avoid drowning or even getting wet... or get in there and learn to surf while the waves of adversity crash on top of you. Life can be scary. Opening up, taking risks and putting yourself out there can be scary. But it's the only way to experience the true beauty that life has to offer! Be fearless, be bold and be authentic! You never know when it's going to pay off, and God will reward your courage. Start a business, express your feelings, pursue a passion, take a trip, and love. Get out of your comfort zone today and start LIVING!

A few days ago, one of my co-workers suffered a massive heart attack. Fortunately, he was in the hospital when it occurred, and he's on his way to a full recovery. However, I already have an issue with focusing excessively on my own mortality. It's not that I'm "scared" of death or anything like that, but the idea that I could pass away on a whim without having completed my mission does bother me.

I have these random thoughts: "What the fuck am I doing right now… is this serving me? Am I wasting my life?" I'm sure we've all had similar thoughts when not honoring ourselves or our time. I'm sharing this because being grounded to this planet is still very much something I struggle with. I can usually sense when it's coming, because I have a strong desire to go fast. I own an SUV, so I'm limited and do not act on this desire, but I love sports cars. I love to go fast, and I love the high that comes with it.

To ground myself, the first thing I do is think consciously about my breathing. I close my eyes, focus on my breathing and begin reciting in my head, "this too shall pass." Typically, when someone starts saying or thinking "this too shall pass," it's because of some dire situation or stress. For me, it's when things are going great as well as when they're looking grim.

All of life is fleeting as fuck. It's the reason I don't filter myself. I would much rather you learn something from the "real" me than the cleaned up, "public" version of me.

The same can be said of the friendships and relationships I have. I love my friends and family. I am sincere to the point of being uncomfortable, because I want everyone to know how much they mean to me. I do not want anyone to think that I take them for granted – even when I'm acting like an asshole.

The life you have is a gift. The wealthiest men and women on this planet are those who have spent their days in complete awareness of this fact and managed to truly "live" until their final breaths.

My co-worker texting me on a Saturday about minor work-related issues, then turning around on Sunday and having a heart attack was a glaring reminder of the fragility of life.

The sacred contract you signed when you came to this place has an expiration date on it that none of us can know. Society as a whole is going to try to tell you how to prioritize and manage your life. As you "score" yourself against others and their successes or failures, the stress that will be placed upon you is enormous.

Stop it. Let it go, for this too shall pass. Your experiences and life are happening right now. You will be conditioned to believe that we're all going to "make it" to an advanced age. This is dangerous thinking. "I'll do it tomorrow, say it tomorrow, act on it tomorrow, apologize tomorrow, visit tomorrow," is one of the most dangerous attitudes to carry.

Your tomorrow could be a drunk driver leaving the bar at 6 p.m. in rush hour traffic, driving head on into your lane. Your tomorrow could be a clogged artery that has gone undetected.

Fuck tomorrow.

Today, right now… this is where it's at. Your life, your mind and your presence change the dynamics of every interaction. Forgive quickly, be gracious and enjoy small things. Love without fear.

I love without boundary; I have no "walls" to speak of. If I had to guess the number one thing that freaks out potential "mates" who are interested in me, it's the realization of this fact (that I don't have a single wall left.) It's cute as they wait for the "other shoe to drop," only to realize it's not happening.

I'm capable of being a massive prick, but so help me God, I do not hold grudges. I thoroughly love to apologize when I'm wrong – especially because it means I get to learn something. My vulnerability and fearless desires to love and be honest are probably my favorite qualities about myself.

Your infinite "good" and your most terrifyingly "bad" will both pass with the sands of time. My mom said to me this morning, "Brenden, try to relax. This moment is but a pebble on the beach of your life."

Thank you, mom. You're both right and wrong. This moment is in fact just a pebble on the beach of my life. The reason is not because my entire life is in front of me, but also because of the incredible life I've left behind me. Everything after today is just a bonus.

As we've learned... this too shall pass.

DARKEST LIGHT BRINGER

A TRIBUTE TO DEBBIE FORD

Life is about moments... the human race has been conditioned to go constantly. Time is rarely allocated for sincere moments of connection or authenticity. Yet, when they do occur, they can bring entire crowds to tears, unifying everyone who is exposed to that moment. The rarity of these moments is what makes them so special. All of mankind lives for these moments.

For many, their most sincere moment is the first time looking into their child's eyes at birth. For others, it's when a long-time goal is finally obtained and conquered. For me, it's the moment my children climb into bed with me, the moment I feel the breeze against my face while walking my dog, or the moment that I lock eyes with someone while engaging in a sincere conversation.

There are thousands of these moments occurring all around us in our day-to-day lives. It only takes you acknowledging them to experience the divinity of life.

I loved Debbie Ford. I never met her, never spoke with her, and in fact had no way of knowing her aside from her books and the light she radiated. Yet, I sincerely loved her. I loved her message, her flaws and her "spirit." Had I met her, I have no doubt we would have been instant friends.

I was introduced to Debbie Ford's work in 2001, when my mom gifted me one of her books, "The Dark Side of the Light Chasers." This book introduced to me a concept that has assisted me personally and continues to be the bedrock of what I teach. The concept is that, yes, you can be a "good" person and pursue dreams, goals and other passions that are positive; however, inside of every single man/woman is a dark side… and that's OK.

As a nineteen year old kid, I struggled mightily with always doing what was "right" and being the best human being possible. It was a constant task as I monitored every thought, action and word I spoke. My biggest problem was that when I was seeking "light" and made a mistake, I was beyond overly critical of myself. I was harsh to the point of depression and anxiety. I hadn't yet realized that being flawed is to be human. Being "whole" and loving the entirety of your "self" is one of the greatest lessons man could ever learn.

Today, this continues to be the number one lesson I share with all of those who will listen. "You must accept that you're not perfect, you will not always be kind, sweet and decent." Both "light" and "darkness" will always be a part of you. Yet, it is in this imperfection that perfection can be discovered.

What you must realize is that the parts of our "self" that are imperfect, ugly and flawed are there to assist in our shaping of empathy, humility and emotional maturity. One would be hard pressed to develop a deep love of their fellow man had they not experienced the stomach-churning guilt associated with shame.

Even the most deplorable, disgusting human being you know, whether it's an ex-lover, boss, friend or whoever… needs a hug.

I'm certainly not condoning shitty behavior or suggesting some pussified society where we all stand in a circle and sing "Kumbaya." But to reject darkness is to reject the whole, and to reject the whole is to only understand half of life.

Having battled her own demons in life, Debbie Ford understood the darkness. Because of her "dark" experiences, she was able to master the ability to bring "light" into her and others' lives. For most people, I think one of the most troubling things about being exposed to darkness is that it serves as a reminder of the work in our own lives that we've yet still to do. It can be demoralizing to observe the social acceptance of deplorable behaviors like violence, infidelity or theft.

For many people, observing darkness causes us to personalize it, as it brings about feelings of guilt for our own shortcomings and mistakes. Debbie Ford believed that we all act as mirrors for one another. She felt that observing the negative in other people caused an emotional response primarily because it mirrored some piece of ourselves that we were ashamed of. However, the converse is true as well: our light can be an inspiration and reminder to those around us of the light they have inside of themselves.

I tend to agree with her. I believe that this concept is the reason committing to a life of self-help and self-evaluation – no matter how many people you've got blowing smoke up your ass, telling you that you "don't need to change" – is critical to the advancement of society.

We cannot forget our own darkness. When you accept your own darkness, it allows others to do the same. The telepathic message is "Yes, even your heroes are fucked up human beings from time to time. It does not make them any less of a person, but it does in fact mean that nobody is without flaw."

One of my heroes (my beautiful mother, Lisa Kitter) was constantly inundated with my criticisms over the years. Not because I didn't love her, but because she was my hero and at the time, I didn't understand the "dark side." I held her to a standard that no human being could live up to, and thusly, she would "let me down" when that weight became too much.

Over the years, and after having come face to face with my own dark side, I realized what I had been doing to my poor mother. I embraced the value of my own "dark side" and thus was able to more willingly accept hers as well. The ultimate irony is that, in getting comfortable with my own shortcomings as a human being, I was able to appreciate that much more of the brilliance of my mother as well as the other people in my life.

When you learn to be "OK" with you, it allows others to be "OK" with themselves. Debbie Ford knew this, and I am so thankful that she took the time to share both her darkness and her light with the world. By putting herself out there so courageously, she helped a nineteen-year-old kid grow into an empathetic, loving man.

CHANNELING YOUR HIGHER SELF

A FUNCTIONAL GUIDE

First, let me explain that what I describe as "channeling" is probably much different than what you THINK I'm referring to. Typically, when someone mentions channeling, it's assumed we're dealing with spirits, ghosts, angels or whatever. However, that is NOT what I am referring to.

One thing that I've learned over the years is that unless you're one hundred percent certain of a fact, DO NOT PUT IT IN WRITING. Otherwise, you risk looking like a colossal asshole and could face serious consequences.

That being said, I *am* one hundred percent certain that I've learned to, at the very least, access information that is for whatever reason stored in a different part of the brain. I cannot say definitively that it's "God," "Universe," "Higher Self," "Collective Unconscious" or any other name it's been given. What I can say is that it's significantly "smarter" than I am, and it seems to yield incredible answers for nearly every single question I ask. (Unfortunately, as of this morning, I have not yet been able to get it to tell me winning lottery numbers… I will continue trying.)

Step #1 – Quiet Your Thoughts

So now that I've done the song and dance to tip toe around the atheists without pissing off the Christians or any other religious group (I'm doing my best to make this explanation as "scientific" as possible,) let's get to the "How-to's" of channeling the wisdom that resides inside of you.

When I first began seriously doing this, I was eighteen years old. I had attended church all of three times, and I really didn't have much of a relationship with the Universe or with myself for that matter. As I began educating myself, I began reading about men/women who had successfully found answers to the majority of their questions through meditation and other means. They almost all spoke of "quieting" their minds so that they could allow the answers to flow toward the front of their mind and into consciousness (channeling.)

Many people have had success just sitting quietly and waiting until the answers arrived. Others try a more active approach by playing music, running water or smoking marijuana.

What I found that worked phenomenally well for me is the following method. I would sit quietly with a notebook and a pen and practice my signature.

Line by line, I would fill the notebook as I practiced my signature (my signature still sucks by the way,) and slowly but surely, the muddled thoughts would begin to dissipate.

It should be noted that my mind never actually went "fully" blank. To this day, I don't think I've ever experienced that feeling while meditating. However, it did slow down long enough for me to get where I needed to go.

After a time of practicing my signature, I would eventually be "unconscious" long enough that a random question would come to mind. Before I could complete the thought, this other aspect of my mind was answering.

I began writing answers before I could even finish writing the question onto my notepad. (It's for this reason that I now use a computer, as I can type much faster than I can write.) The very first time it happened, I was hooked. I knew I had unlocked a part of myself that I had never experienced.

Step #2 – Trust

The first time I did this exercise, it took me a solid forty-five minutes for anything to happen. However, once it began happening, I did not question it during the session.

Yes, I did go back and read what I had written down and question afterward. I was blown away! I didn't know what the hell to make of the information I had written.

You're going to experience something similar the first time you channel the deeper parts of your mind. You might be surprised at what you find, and you'll wonder how it got there.

It's OK to have feelings of skepticism and confusion.

However, as you continue practicing your new skill and willingly delve into the deepest parts of your psyche, you will come to truly know yourself. I firmly believe it was during those early sessions that I not only found "me," but also fell in love with "me."

Step #3 – Document the Experience

Initially, you're more than likely going to think you're going insane. That's normal. I walked around for a month going, "Holy shit! What the fuck is happening to me?!"

This is not something that you're taught in school or church, and unless you've got some super badass parents, probably not at home. This journey you're on of self-improvement, enlightenment or whatever the kids are calling it these days is a very "personal" experience. Rarely in the past have people openly guided others toward these types of endeavors.

The reason I'm sharing so much of this information and asking you to document it is because you never know what you're going to find. Inside of one of your answers may lie the "truth" that someone is seeking. It could be one of the most profound thoughts you've ever had, and we do NOT want this to be something that is fleeting.

Document everything. It's not so you can "validate" it to other people – but believe me, they'll ask for "proof" if you tell them about your new hobby. The documentation is for YOU. Your analytical/ego mind is going to try to make you doubt your own wisdom. You can combat those thoughts by documenting the experience thoroughly.

Step #4 – Practice

Now I'm not going to say some cliché shit like "practice makes
perfect." I will, however, say that meditating in general is good for
you. If during that meditation, you're able to glean bits of wisdom,
I see no harm in that. The more you make both a conscious and
unconscious effort, the more you'll be able to tap into this part of
the brain.

I've been doing this for the better part of thirteen years, and I am
at a point that if I'm in front of a computer and you ask a question,
I can call upon that part of my mind at will.

Believe me… I'd love to tell you that I'm just that "smart" and all
of the wisdom and content I share came from my "education." I'd
be lying my ass off if I told you that! I am not unique in being able
to do this, and with a commitment to practice, you can easily
replicate or even exceed my results.

Step #5 – Personalize the Experience

Not everyone is going to sit down at a computer and do what I do.
Nor is everyone going to want to practice their signature until they
begin talking to themselves and getting amazing answers. Many of
you will think this is ridiculous and will be skeptical that it's
possible to access these parts of your own mind. I'm fine with that.

I'll still be the one you text/email/call when the shit hits the fan in your life and you need help. Live. Laugh. Love!

What you have to remember is that you can ALL do this in a method that is particularly close to you. I strongly suggest implementing these types of dialogues into your method of communication. Some of you are musicians, so the dialogue may come while creating music.

Others might be handymen or mechanics who work with their hands. I'm not much of a handyman, but the times that I've had to work with my hands, I've enjoyed turning off the music and being alone with my thoughts. There is silence in those moments that even the most skeptical of "manly men" enjoy.

WHAT IS YOUR LEGACY?

From time to time, I wake up with an overwhelming sense of my own mortality. It's not that I obsess about "dying" or anything of that nature. Rather, I have a healthy appreciation for just how fleeting life can be and the legacy I'm leaving behind. I'm a firm believer that it's an important and healthy practice to rejoice and give thanks for every single day that you wake up. It's equally important to know that much of what happens in this life in regards to living and dying is beyond our control.

Every single day, we're inundated with news of people passing prematurely, abruptly and without warning. Dying is a major part of living. I do not fear death simply because I know that it's the natural progression of the human experience.

However, I promised myself long ago that I wouldn't be someone who finds himself in his final moments "wishing" he had done more, said more, expressed more or experienced more. My legacy is firmly cultivated in my beautiful children, my writing and in the relationships I've formed during my life.

Sharing this is not meant to be a "downer." I'm simply trying to get the point across that none of us know when we'll be taken. We don't know when our loved ones, friends, husband, wife or boss are going to finish their time on this planet and be gone. You do not have time to waste on being angry, bitter or guarded.

Most people who deal with me are taken aback by my sincerity. If I'm upset with you... you'll know. If I care about you, it'll never be something you have to question.

Some people are equipped with a sense of fear about getting hurt emotionally; I am not one of those people. I love deeply. I'm not wired to hold back or to be cautious. I'm fully aware of my own mortality, and as such, I make sure everyone who participates in my life (even in a minor capacity) knows that I love and appreciate them.

God willing, my legacy of spreading love and positivity in an honest and sincere manner will last long after my death. I've reached a place in my life where I no longer seek love; rather, I am love. The euphoria that goes along with the feeling of falling in love is what I experience throughout my days. I am completely in love with the process of life.

Falling in love with life is what has allowed me to move past depression, anxiety and other debilitating issues that many face. Falling in love with life and my legacy has allowed me to act with a sense of purpose and passion every single day.

I hadn't planned on covering this topic, but some asshole decided to do something using the lowest form of human expression, causing a disturbance in the force, and I feel a metaphysical obligation to create context for the senseless violence that occurred at the Boston Marathon.

Throughout human history, violence has been used to deal with issues where the minds of men/women have failed. An unwillingness to slow down and think rationally is instead replaced with fear, irrational behavior and callousness.

Today, thanks to technology and the sharing of ideas and advancements in modern man, even suggesting violence as a viable solution is generally met with uneasiness. I am an aggressive, passionate man, and yet I find myself completely uncomfortable with the idea of inflicting devastating pain on another human being. I've had to defend myself and fight for reasons that were mostly out of my control when I was younger. However, the idea of using such methods today seems about as foreign to me as smoking cigarettes.

One of the beautiful things about Universal Mind or "Gaia" is that this force will advance and evolve as one. What this means is that ideas, emotions and thoughts can be shared, drawn upon and expressed through one voice. Technology and the internet in particular are literally the Global Conscience. Energy exists in addition to billions of thoughts, emotions and ideas, which travel through the internet into our own minds in seconds.

At this very moment, you're reading my thoughts as I lay them out for you, and the parts that resonate as "true" for you are sticking in your subconscious mind. That is the power of "Gaia." I mention this because on a global level, the tolerance for violence grows less and less every single day. The events at the Boston Marathon were fortunate to have only claimed three lives (though it was three too many.) However, the collective response in the immediate wake of such an event was extreme empathy and disappointment.

It was not "terror," like those who perpetrated the monstrosity had hoped. I am no more fearful of attending a sporting event today than I was last week or last year. I do not believe the Global

Conscience is either. Will we be "aware" and "vigilant?" Yes. Are we afraid? Fuck no.

The act of using violence to elicit an emotional response of fear and distrust is dying. The human unconscious is moving past this line of thought and energy. God bless those that were affected directly. The pictures were horrific, and yet, amongst the mayhem, I saw beauty.

The initial reaction from those present at the time of that explosion was not to turn and run. Instead, there was an immediate reaction and unconscious desire to help those who were most affected.

This is not normal for mass groups of people. We've seen violence before that resulted in death, injury and widespread panic. For the most part, I did not see panic, but rather determination and compassion. Mankind... I am impressed. We would be naive to think that the old paradigm would go quietly. It will not. This will not be the last act of senseless, disgusting violence. However, the reaction by the Global Conscience suggests that such behavior is becoming less and less effective at "herding" people toward fear.

Our resolve and unwillingness to be "scared" disempowers those who seek control via intimidation and fear. Our collective faith in one another and our ability to overcome anything as a species run counter to the reaction they're hoping for. When you cease to incentivize your enemy, the enemy will cease to attack. That mode of thought and action is no longer effective.

Violence is losing its power. Man is moving toward significantly brighter days. While such tragedies remain fresh in the collective conscious, I would implore everyone to focus on the reaction of your fellow man rather than the action of a few twisted individuals.

WHY MOST FITNESS EFFORTS FAIL

AND WHAT YOU CAN DO TO SUCCEED

Being able to look at yourself with reverence and sincere appreciation is critical to honoring your temple. Excessive alcohol, drugs, casual sex with multiple partners or high sugar/low nutrient-dense foods will also adversely affect the spiritual connection you have with your body, especially giving away your sexual energy. Harnessing that power can lead you to success in business as well as attracting quality relationships. Men and women who give away this energy to unworthy partners are left with a dim life force.

How many times have you sat down and said, "Today is the day I start exercising, eating right and living a more healthy life?" Almost all of us have at some point.

Our intentions are good. We want to look and feel healthier. Sometimes, it's to recapture part of our youth. Other times, it's out of necessity. A number of people stay naturally slim for years, only to realize in their thirties and forties that a sedentary lifestyle and slow metabolism can defeat even the best genetics. So begins the cycle of fad dieting and new workout crazes.

The first thing most people do upon starting a fitness plan or diet is go to "old reliable" for knowledge. No, not a certified personal trainer or fitness enthusiast – they go to the "other" expert… Google. Search after search yields diet pill after diet pill. Maybe you get lucky and you do find a site that has some information on "calories in vs. calories out" or "nutrition made easy."

While this information is useful, it doesn't prepare you for the task that awaits you. There is a science and methodology to everything. Most people are going to tell you that "their way" of doing things is the best. So called "fitness experts" are going to try to sell you on a multitude of different gimmicks and quick fixes.

There are no quick fixes that have lasting results. Hard work, dedication and discipline are the only long-term solution for maintaining a healthy and fit body. Now before you get depressed and give up, because you realize you are neither dedicated nor disciplined, listen up. You can do this if you break it down into steps. Any fitness goal – and I mean ANY – can be accomplished if you're willing to earn it.

When most people decide they're going to have a six pack in three weeks, this is what goes through their minds:

"I am going to be ripped! First, I'm going to go buy a gym membership, then I'll buy some fat burners. After that, it's off to Trader Joe's to buy organic soy milk and a box of cardboard... err, I mean rice cakes! I'll be ripped in NO TIME!"

For those who don't think like the above, their thought process usually looks something like this:

"I really need to lose weight. My doctor says my weight is causing high blood pressure. Maybe I'll call one of those personal trainers whose ad I saw on Google... but I'm too big to get in shape..."

Both of these trains of thought are destined for failure.

The first person is absolutely sky high about getting in shape. They "think" they've got it all figured out, and that it's not going to be difficult. The problem is that the motivation they are feeling will wear off – especially when they don't see the results they're expecting within the first couple of weeks. The other problem is that they've immediately started a ridiculous diet that is nearly impossible to maintain.

The average human being cannot change years and years of habits on a whim. It doesn't work that way. Long-term, lasting results are discovered through gradual and systematic change over the course of time. (There are those rare exceptions who will be able to make these changes on a whim. Odds are: you are not one of them.)

The second person in our example is the one who doesn't believe that fitness is even possible. This person is considering change solely because their doctor said it was paramount to their survival. They have yet to confront themselves honestly; therefore, they have a skewed view of reality. The good news is that they contemplated getting a professional trainer to help. The bad news is that believing they will fail will probably prevent them from following through.

The solution to both of these problems is simple: be honest with yourself. If you're obese or overweight, accept it. You did it to yourself. It wasn't McDonald's. It wasn't your mom or dad's lack of love. It wasn't the bully or the failed relationship. It was you.

Maybe you're a busy professional who is responsible for many important decisions, and you also have a household to run. Sorry, it's still your fault.

No matter what excuse you come up with, I'm telling you right now that it was your fault. I've never heard of someone holding a gun to anyone's head and forcing them to inhale a Big Mac and fries.

Now that we've been honest with ourselves and taken responsibility for our actions, we can move on to the next step of the process... change. First we're going to realize that it took years to get this big and it may take years to get it off. You have to accept that. Can it all come off in months? In some cases, yes. Will it? Who knows? It doesn't matter anyway; you have made the decision to get in shape and be healthy for the long haul. Once you've drawn your proverbial line in the sand, whether it takes months or years is irrelevant.

Fitness is a journey, not a destination. There are more than a few once proud bodybuilders (who had sported six pack abs and twenty inch guns for most of their twenties and thirties,) who now, at the age of forty-five, can't see their feet. Don't let this be you. It's a journey, not a destination.

The following is something I did with MY clients. It does not mean it is the gospel or is the only way to achieve great results. This is a method that has worked for me, and that's why I'm sharing it.

If you have not been a part of health and fitness of any kind for months, years or ever... listen up. I DO NOT RECOMMEND

STARTING A NUTRITION PROGRAM AT THE SAME TIME YOU BEGIN EXERCISING. Now you're probably thinking, "What the hell is this guy talking about?" Remember when I said that it's a gradual and systematic change?

Most clients that I've had who started out with a training program that called for exercise three times per week in addition to a meal plan right out the gate… failed. It's too much to ask of yourself to completely overhaul who you are in a matter of days.

My rule is that we begin training and exercising for three weeks before I'll even discuss nutrition. Even if you just exercised and did not alter your eating at all during the first three weeks, you are still going to see some results. I would rather the client feel a sense of accomplishment after three weeks than feel disappointment the first time they mess up on their meal plan.

By the third week, my clients are usually begging for nutritional advice, which is the reason I do it. They change at their own pace. I didn't force them to give up their entire identity and change in a millisecond.

If you're not working with a personal trainer, I would still recommend not thinking at all about your diet for the first three weeks. Allow yourself the opportunity to just focus on exercising three days a week, for an hour each day.

There is more than enough information for you to study about exercise to keep you busy the first three weeks. Once you've been to the gym at least three times per week for three weeks, then you can start focusing on the diet.

The purpose of this chapter is not to lay out an exact workout program or proper diet. Those are two subjects that are very specific to the individual. I would rather focus on the psychology of fitness and how to develop that discipline.

Like I said before, there are many roads to living a healthy and fit lifestyle. None of them are wrong or right. Some may be safer and more effective than others, but when you are first starting out, it's more important that you're doing something as opposed to nothing – regardless of what that something is.

After you've been attending the gym for a while and have begun some form of meal planning or diet, you will have some hurdles. Maybe you missed a workout or forgot to plan your meals and went through the drive through. Do not panic. You must allow yourself the freedom to make mistakes. Life is demanding and stressful. If you had an off week, accept it and focus on the next week.

In the past thirteen years of personal training, I have had many clients who would not allow themselves the chance to slip up. As a result, they were constantly riding a wave of ups and downs.

Eventually, they couldn't take it anymore and quit. That is not a realistic way to live. Fitness is not just about getting stronger physically; it's about mental strength as well. It takes mental strength to not be perfect but still strive for perfection.

You can achieve your fitness goals. It's not going to be easy, but it may become easier as time goes on. You are responsible for your current physical state. No family member, boss or friend "made" you fat. You have accepted this and are now changing.

Your initial goal is to exercise three days per week, for an hour each day... for three weeks. You will then start slowly implementing some form of meal plan and/or nutritional rules.

You're going to have hurdles that you must overcome and forgive yourself for making. This journey is for the long haul, and you realize that even though you may slip up sometimes, you will not give up. You deserve to look and feel healthier.

Body Dysmorphia

Ladies, you've got to stop with this shit. Bodybuilding, fitness and eating healthy are not about developing an OCD-like complex for food or the gym. Body dysmorphia can be extremely dangerous when it's not addressed.

Real talk, this shit isn't funny anymore. All of the duck-faced and tits-out pictures aren't validating anything. You're only perpetuating the degradation of your already fragile self image.

If you're going to eat healthy and compete, that's awesome! However, do it for the right reasons and more importantly, stay with it because it's something you enjoy. Your negative self-image doesn't have to be permanent.

Y'all are beautiful already. "Men" love curves, hips and feminine bodies! I'll happily take a woman who's a hundred percent comfortable in her own skin but is carrying an extra ten pounds over some woman I fear I might snap in half during sex.

There is no more important "workout" than the one you do in front of the mirror every morning. That four-inch space between your ears is going to have a far bigger impact on your "results" than any number of squats! I'm not standing on my soap box without experience… as a personal trainer, I mastered the psychology of fitness.

Throughout my career, I had many clients with body dysmorphia. I'd say over ninety percent of my clients look better now than they did when I trained them, thanks to our ability to effectively address body dysmorphia issues. I pride myself in flipping the switch subconsciously in my clients and unlocking the potential for a lifetime of results.

How did I do that, you may ask?

- Positive affirmation daily
- Preaching forgiveness of thyself
- Simplicity
- Instilling self-belief through small successes

It all starts and ends with self-love. You don't get self-love AFTER you get the body. Develop the love first, and as a result, the desired body is achieved. Body dysmorphia can be incredibly debilitating if not addressed. To all of you men and women who suffer from this disease, please remember that you're not alone. It's far more prevalent than you might think.

SELF-ACTUALIZATION

THE ANSWERS LIE WITHIN

Take a moment of silence to say goodbye to the previous version of yourself. Every morning, we wake up born anew and reflect briefly on the person who died the night before. We forgive that person for their flaws and lack of strength. We thank that person for having survived the day so that you might wake up today, smarter, stronger and wiser.

The suffering died with the old you last night. This morning is your chance to start anew… to start with a clean slate. If you need to apologize for things that person did yesterday, then do so. However, now is the time to move forward humbly with focus and INTEGRITY in your life. Today is your day to conquer that man/woman's demons from the previous day. Today is the day you stop being scared, and you let go of all that does not serve your life in a positive way.

Self-Actualization – "the achievement of one's full potential through creativity, independence, spontaneity and a grasp of the real world"

Or

"The process of establishing oneself as a whole person, able to develop one's abilities and to understand oneself"

What a beautiful term. I was speaking with a friend recently, and she and I were discussing the emphasis as of late (through social media, television and other means,) on the idea that people all need to be "more" than they already are.

Musicians, artists, actors, authors, speakers and the list goes on and on of people who are telling you that you aren't good enough and need to change. Many of them speak of "enlightenment" and "growth" as destinations that can be achieved – especially if you buy their products!

The truth is that all of you out there already are the person you wish to experience. "Enlightenment, success, fitness, good health and sexy, smart, rich, funny, confident" are all terms that currently occupy a place within you. Through self-actualization, they can be realized.

There is no money in telling you that you already "are" that which you wish to be. There is no way to sell you a solution or a series of solutions if you're aware of these facts.

I'm not saying that many of these authors (hell, I am one!) don't have value to offer you. Perhaps you're seeking a partner or teacher in this process, as many of us have sought throughout history.

However, the greatest truth you could ever find within is that you are and have always been that which you seek. Having this moment of self-actualization is what can and does unlock your unlimited potential as a person. In that moment, it ceases being "potential" and becomes your "I am."

Before I was the best personal trainer I could be, I was an eighteen-year-old kid with zero work experience and limited fitness experience outside of weightlifting from playing football. I hadn't ever put together a workout program or studied any anatomy.

I did, however, have something that is rarely found in the personal training industry… I had the ability to project my will and self-esteem onto others. I could make them "believe" in themselves and in fitness, believing is ninety percent of the equation.

I was fortunate to have been mentored by a brilliant manager named Kevin Hughes. He taught me more about projecting enthusiasm and confidence onto clients than anyone in my entire career. Kevin was a phenomenal trainer because he had an infectious attitude that made people want to participate.

The gym where I worked was one hundred percent sink or swim. They were hiring and firing five to six trainers per month.

My first day of employment began on my eighteenth birthday; I signed my paperwork after I finished school that afternoon. I wasn't going to be afforded any kind of "practice" time.

Kevin immediately put me so far out of my comfort zone that to this day, I'm convinced it's the reason I've learned to love awkward situations. He placed me and a co-worker at the entrance and had us working a booth. We were asked to hand out sample protein bars to guests coming into the club.

This went on for about an hour and was pretty easy. I wasn't too nervous, and after the first few guests, it felt quite natural. Kevin, being the ever-challenging mentor that he was, could tell we were getting used to the task.

"Hey guys, we're going to switch things up. One of you is going to stay here, and the other one is going to go on the workout floor and introduce yourself to ten people. You must come back after having met ten people, and you must remember their names."

Goodbye, comfort zone.

This was going to be awkward as fuck. I was a fairly intelligent and charismatic guy, but up until this point, I had struggled with this type of activity. My co-worker was a much more outgoing person and jumped right into the task.

I watched as he circled the gym introducing himself and shaking the hands of strangers. I was in awe. Could I do such a thing? Would I stumble over my words? Perhaps the members wouldn't take me seriously?

My mind was racing with fears and insecurities. Finally, it was my turn. I took a deep breath and headed out into the wild. The first conversation got off to a rocky start to say the least.

"S-s-sup. I'm Brenden," I stuttered. "Who are you?"

Clearly annoyed, the random smoking-hot cardio bunny replied, "Excuse me?"

"I... I umm... I work here. What's your name?"

"That's nice. I'm trying to work out," she snapped as she stared blankly ahead.

Eeeeend scene.

Fuuuuuuuuuuck!

That was awkward just typing it and then reading it, let alone having LIVED it. I went back to Kevin and said, "Man, I don't think I'm going to be able to do this." Kevin told me to "stop over-thinking simple exchanges with people." The key was to not have an agenda and to just be myself. He wasn't going to let me off of the hook, and so I did what he told me and went back out.

My next few exchanges got better, and I was beginning to relax. I started visualizing not how the members would respond, but rather who it was I wanted them to see me as. I projected myself as a strong, seasoned personal trainer who had the answers to their life questions.

1, 2, 3, 4, 5, 6, 7, 8, 9...

The conversations and the names were happening quickly and easily. I still had one last name to collect and knew who I wanted to talk to… the smoking hot cardio bunny.

With an air of confidence, I marched toward her on the treadmill. She must have seen me coming, because she was trying to look anywhere but in my direction. I didn't give a shit. She was going to talk to me and give me her name, or I was prepared to make this the most awkward cardio session of her life.

"Well hello, again!" I started.

"Ugh… you again?"

"Hey, remember that time I walked up to you and nearly pissed myself while asking for your name?"

"Yes. That was like twenty minutes ago."

"Well in the last twenty minutes, I decided I'm the best personal trainer in this club, and I insist on knowing all of my members' names. What's your name?"

Staring at me blankly, mouth slightly agape, she answered, "I'm… I'm Tiffany."

"Nice to meet you, Tiffany. I'm not sure what your fitness goals are, or if you're just in here picking up dudes or whatever, but I'd love to help you out. What time are you available for a free consultation?"

Her demeanor softening, she replied, "I can sit down with you after I'm done doing my cardio… if that's OK?"

"That would be perfect. I'll come back here in ten minutes as you're finishing up and grab you."

On that day, I learned a valuable lesson and inadvertently stumbled upon self-actualization. Becoming the best personal trainer I was capable of being wasn't going to be a two to three-year endeavor. Obviously, I got better with experience and knowledge. However, that afternoon, I developed the swagger, confidence, will and undying belief necessary to grow into the best personal trainer I could be.

This was my first moment of self-actualization. Time and time again, I've replicated that moment in different phases of my life.

STILL BREATHIN'...

"I don't see myself being special; I just see myself having more responsibilities than the next man. People look to me to do things for them, to have answers." Tupac Shakur

I can't tell you if this is the beginning or the end. What I can tell you is that everything you have read thus far is thirty-one years of love, hate, struggle, pain, pleasure, family, friends, enemies, success, failure, truth, lies, shame and faith. It's my desire that this be the beginning. It's my belief that as I grow, so too will my writing. However, if this was it, if the book you have just read and experienced was my final stamp on this world, I could die a happy man.

Much of the world tiptoes quietly through life for fear of judgement, failure and pain. You deserve to express yourself. You deserve to create and experience this journey in every capacity. Every single day, beautiful souls are taken prematurely and without notice – beautiful souls who had waited for "the perfect time" or the "perfect person" to come along so that they might start living the lives they'd always dreamed.

Do not trust the future. Do not assume that you've got a tomorrow. Life is a beautiful tapestry of events, emotions and thoughts. It is not meant to be simply "observed." Rather, you should be exploring the depths of your humanity, daily. Live fearlessly and stand in the face of your own self-doubt and laugh.

Whether you acknowledge your responsibility on this planet to discover peace, happiness and purpose is irrelevant; it remains true. We're all in this life together, and your thoughts, actions and willingness to risk everything for the sake of a purpose-driven life is the greatest gift you can offer the world.

Teach your children to persevere through your failures. Teach your friends to believe through your success. Teach your enemies to forgive through your empathy. Teach the world to love through your vulnerability. Teach your family to trust through your loyalty, and teach yourself to have faith through your experience.

FREQUENT QUESTIONS

AND ANSWERS

"I don't ever feel like I'm doing enough. So, when my me time comes along, I feel guilty."

The person asking the first question is a married woman who has children and a full time job. Feelings like this are totally normal, but they do speak of an underlying issue that must be addressed. Many of us struggle with feeling that we're "not doing enough." It's my opinion that there are a handful of reasons for this.

1) You've been conditioned to "Go! Go! Go!" and so when it's finally time to actually relax and treat yourself, you've got no clue how to do it. I think a lot of mothers in particular suffer from this, because multi-tasking is in your nature. Unfortunately, if you maintain this pace for too long without treating yourself, it wears on you and you start becoming difficult to get along with.

2) You're not pursuing your life's "purpose"; therefore, you are always left with a feeling of dissatisfaction and/or guilt associated with that with which you're working on.

My feeling on the woman above is that she's more of #1. She's a phenomenal mother and loves her career, so I don't think that she's feeling like she's not pursuing her passions. However, her life is not completely in alignment as she's feeling "guilty" for doing things for herself. I suffered from this for YEARS.

Everything was always about the kids, especially when I was on that poverty time. I got into a routine of always putting the needs of the children and my bills over my own. There was a point when I bought myself a pair of shoes only once every two years because I couldn't handle the guilt associated with the purchase. Slowly, over the last two years, I've conquered this.

While I still pay my bills and definitely spoil all of my children and visit my daughters in California consistently, the difference is that I now make sure to stay in harmony with my own needs and desires. I treat myself to small purchases and don't feel any guilt at all. I won't lie… it took practice.

I think the majority of that "guilt" comes from a feeling of "not enough" or a scarcity mindset. I had been poor for so long that once I finally achieved a little financial success, I was terrified that as soon as I spent money on myself, things would fall apart, and I'd find myself needing that money back. This is a totally fucked up way of looking at things, and yet the majority of us operate that way.

There IS enough.

Honoring yourself isn't irresponsible; it's imperative for leading a happy, balanced life. If you ignore your desires and allow the guilt to control you, you'll eventually come to resent your job, life and responsibilities.

"What do I do about a man who works too much and whose job continuously takes him away from me, not allowing for a relationship?"

The short answer… find a new man. The person asking this question originally suggested that I write a chapter on how "men can balance a career and relationship," rather than asking me what to do. I, being the blunt prick that I am, simply said, "He's either married or fucking other people."

However, she does pose an interesting question that I'm sure many female readers have had. While I'm sure that there are men out there who struggle with balance much like women do, the truth is that we DO prioritize our relationships… when we see the relationship as something of value.

If someone isn't making you a priority, it means that the feelings aren't deep enough to do so. No man is THAT busy that he's not able to stop working to spend time with you. All that is, is a convenient excuse to not see you. Hell, the same goes for people with kids. "Oh, I can't see you because I've got kids." What kind of weak-ass excuse is that? When people want something, they'll make it happen. Anything else is just bullshit.

The truth is that they're just trying to be nice. They don't want to hurt your feelings, or perhaps you're providing them something that they don't want to lose, but they aren't willing to prioritize your relationship because the sex is all they want.

What you've got to ask yourself is this… why would anyone pursue someone like that? It seems like a colossal waste of time and causes a lot of heartache. Men/women need to do less "fixing" of the people they're trying to be with and focus instead on attracting individuals that don't need fixing.

This next question comes from a reader who is an absolute sweetheart to me. She's had her critiques and criticisms over the years, but she always does so in such a thoughtful way that I can't help but consider her opinion valuable.

"Brenden! I hope you don't take offense to this message and know I have the most honest and genuine intentions when writing to you. I know you want a "good girl" from your writing; I clearly see you're searching for that. I see you don't like the "ratchets" and other terms you use to describe the women who I am assuming approach you often. But the way you portray yourself is, in my opinion, somewhat arrogant and chauvinistic..."

The short answer... I'm somewhat arrogant and chauvinistic.

The long answer... My favorite kind of humor is taking words/thoughts/opinions that are extremely taboo and making fun of them. I also do my best to be fair and make fun of people equally so that nobody feels left out or alienated.

My goal isn't to be "politically correct." My goal is not to present myself as "perfect" or without flaws. I am capable of being an asshole of epic proportions. Believe me; I'm fully aware of these weaknesses. As a writer, all I can hope for is to provoke thought. I'll happily be the biggest douchebag, asshole chauvinist you ladies ever met, if it means you're reading, learning and becoming empowered.

I'm not here trying to land a wife with my words. I'm trying to teach you something and hold your attention long enough to elicit positive change. The exchange we make every time you read my material is this... I give you my vulnerability, flaws, wisdom and humor. In exchange, you give me your attention, your mind and an opportunity to teach you something. If your opinions of me are diminished from reading my content, BUT you're leading happier lives from something you learned herein... I'll take that exchange all day, every day.

I've got this written on the back of this book and perhaps some of you haven't seen it or read it. For that reason, I'm putting it here again:

"I am far from a perfect man. I am flawed. I've made mistakes. I don't know it all. I am, by my very nature, somewhat superficial. I love smart, beautiful women. I love fast cars, good vodka and power. I am no expert in love or business. I am, however, an expert in the human experience and condition. There is not much in the adversity department that I haven't seen or done. Poverty, divorce, humility, shame, joy, love, success, failure – been there, done it.

Character, balance, honesty, romance, parenting, faith… these are my most valuable traits. I'm the best friend you never had, the brother you always wanted, the lover you fantasized about, enemy you hate, child you're proud of, man you're disappointed in. I am you… I'm your good, bad, beauty and ugliness all at the same time. I am a fighter, a lover, the Yin and the Yang. I am the teacher, the student and most importantly… I am Whole."

ABOUT THE AUTHOR

He comes on strong; he has no filter,
He can see your soul; there is no shelter.
Honesty that's appreciated,
Until it's directed at you,
Loyalty everlasting, and limited to few.

Brenden Dilley was introduced to the world of "self-help" at the age of eleven by his mother, Lisa Kitter. At the age of thirteen, he was doing book reports on titles such as "Think and Grow Rich" by Napoleon Hill. He was raised in a typical middle-class family until his parents divorced when he was thirteen. His mother would later become a self-made millionaire as a speaker, author and corporate trainer. During this time Brenden worked, traveled, spoke and mentored by his mom's side.

Upon graduating from high school, Brenden would go on to become a highly successful personal trainer, receiving his certification through the National Academy of Sports Medicine. However, Brenden wasn't content with simply parroting the teachings of others. He would eventually create his class and method of training called "The Psychology of Fitness." Utilizing this unique form of self-development and body altering training, Brenden became known for transforming client's bodies as well as their minds. It was widely known that if you committed to training with Brenden not only would you become healthier physically, but other facets of your life would improve as well.

Brenden is also a single parent to his three children: Sophia Rose, Jasmine Nai'a and Phoenix Alexander. Much of what Brenden writes, speaks about, teaches and trains on revolves around parenting, dating, relationships, self-empowerment, fitness and authenticity. His intensity, intelligence, directness and self-deprecating humor allow audiences and readers to relate to him on a very raw and authentic level.

Brenden speaks fearlessly to his audience, rarely ever pulling punches, yet at the same time making himself one hundred percent vulnerable so that his intentions are crystal clear. He's pouring out his pain and wisdom for the benefit of others.

Currently, Brenden resides in Gilbert, Arizona, and works in the world of commercial real estate development, where his unique skill set as both a leader, manager and problem solver are utilized in the fast-paced world of multi-family housing development.

Brenden's innate ability to cultivate strong relationships while problem solving through innovative methods and his background as a single parent, personal development fitness trainer and fast-paced corporate shark make putting him into a "box" of any sort nearly impossible.

Find Brenden Dilley online:

http://www.brendendilley.com
http://www.youtube.com/hublife
http://www.twitter.com/hublife
http://www.facebook.com/brendendilley
http://www.facebook.com/stillbreathinbook
http://www.instagram.com/brenden_dilley

Made in the USA
Middletown, DE
12 July 2020